BASEMENT
IDEAS THAT WORK

BASEMENT
IDEAS THAT WORK
Creative design solutions for your home

PETER JESWALD

The Taunton Press

Text © 2007 by The Taunton Press, Inc.
Illustrations © 2007 by The Taunton Press, Inc.
All rights reserved.

 The Taunton Press
Inspiration for hands-on living®

The Taunton Press, Inc.,
63 South Main Street, PO Box 5506,
Newtown, CT 06470-5506
e-mail: tp@taunton.com

Interior design: Carol Petro
Layout: Lissi Sigillo
Illustrator: Christine Erikson
Front cover photos: (top, left to right) © Eric Roth; Photo courtesy Owens-Corning;
© Tim Lee; © Eric Roth; (bottom, clockwise from left) © Jessie Walker Associates;
© Mark Lohman; © Mark Lohman; © Tim Lee
Front flap photo: © Mark Lohman
Back cover photos (top, left to right) © David Schrock/Basement Spaces, Inc.; © Tim
Street Porter; © Eric Roth; © Olsen Photographic; (middle) © Mark Lohman Photogra-
phy; (bottom, left to right) © Mark Samu, Samu Studios; © Mark Lohman
Back flap photos: (clockwise from top left) © Carolyn Bates, carolynbates.com; © David
Schrock/Basement Spaces, Inc.; © Alise O'Brien; © Mark Samu, Samu Studios

Library of Congress Cataloging-in-Publication Data
Jeswald, Peter.
  Basement ideas that work : creative design solutions for your home / Peter Jeswald.
      p. cm.
  Includes bibliographical references and index.
  ISBN 978-1-56158-937-1 (alk. paper)
  1. Basements–Remodeling. I. Title.

TH4816.3.B35J47 2007
643'.5–dc22
                                                         2007006879

Printed in China
10 9 8 7 6 5 4 3 2 1

The following manufacturers/names appearing in *Basement Ideas that Work* are
trademarks: Ping-Pong®, Play-Doh®, Plexiglas®, Tencil®

ACKNOWLEDGMENTS

I begin by thanking Carolyn Mandarano, senior editor at Taunton Press, who was a pleasure to work with and consistently demonstrated her experience, expertise, and ability to work collaboratively.

I thank the following people for taking time out of their busy schedules to answer my questions and share their insights: Paul Eldrenkamp, Byggmeister Design/Build, Inc.; Stephen Greenwald, Renaissance Builder, Inc.; Sylvain Côté, Absolute Remodeling Corp.; David S. Schrock, Basement Spaces, Inc.; Jim Eggert, Eggert Construction, LLC; Darryl Myers, Abilities Unlimited; and Russell Crenshaw, Cowls Building Supply, Inc.

Finally, I thank my wife, Phyllis Jeswald, for helping me get through a few rough patches.

CONTENTS

INTRODUCTION

Let's face it. When it comes to remodeling, basements often don't get much respect. But given the way basements have been treated in the past, it's easy to see why. Viewed as cheap space, most basements were literally done "on-the-cheap." Design and space layout were virtually ignored. Little attention was paid to the unique requirements of basement construction. And most of the materials installed in basements looked like leftovers from bargain bins. As a result, many basements were just not inviting places. Over time, they reverted to their previous function as storage depots.

Perhaps motivated by increasing home prices and construction costs, homeowners and builders have begun to take a fresh look at basements. Time is now spent thinking about how to effectively use basement space. Advances in building science provide an understanding of proper basement construction techniques. And quality materials are becoming the rule, not an exception. After all, you wouldn't use inferior materials in a kitchen or bathroom remodel, so why should a basement be treated any differently?

Is your home bursting at the seams, every nook and cranny filled by your growing family? Do your children need a place to get away from their parents—or vice versa? Perhaps you'd like to telecommute and need a home office. What about a place to exercise so you can keep up with your kids? You've thought about moving, but you love the neighborhood and the schools. Rearranging the furniture won't solve the problems: You definitely need more space. Building an addition seems like the best solution. Or is it?

Basement Ideas That Work shows you that a better answer may be right under your nose. The following pages will change your image of basements forever. In fact, you might turn a page and find yourself exclaiming, "That can't be a basement." You'll see that basements can accommodate almost every housing need or activity you might have. And there's a lot of nitty-gritty information that will help you determine if remodeling your basement makes sense for you. Even if you're already sold on a basement remodel, *Basement Ideas That Work* has something for you. In addition to inspiration, this book provides you with tricks and techniques to overcome the special challenges basements present.

So set aside your preconceived notions of what remodeled basements used to be and enjoy a tour through the world of the up-to-date basement.

FROM

It may not look like it, but your basement is a gem just waiting to be unearthed,

shaped, polished, and transformed into one the most enjoyable places in your home.

STORAGE TO

But to accomplish this you must be prepared to wrest control of your basement

from the stacks of cardboard boxes that are in the way.

LIVING SPACE

Transforming Your Basement

If you find yourself needing more living space, remodeling your basement may be just the answer. Sure it might be crawling with pipes, wires, and ducts and alive with sounds of mechanical equipment, flushing water, and perhaps an uninvited rodent or two. But don't be so hasty in dismissing this space. Basements have more going for them than meets the eye. Remodeling a typical basement can substantially increase the size of your home.

Compared to building out with an addition that gobbles up precious outdoor space or building up by adding a second floor, remodeling down has some distinct advantages.

With a basement, you don't have to worry about integrating the design into the existing rooflines, as you do when adding a second story, or dealing with setback issues and zoning regulations, as you might with building an addition. And because basements already have foundations, rough walls, and ceilings, builders can work in any kind of weather. Disruptions, unfortunately, are inevitable with any construction project, but they typically are less intense with basement remodels. There's hammering, to be sure, but no one is pounding directly over your head. With basements that have access to the outdoors, workers virtually never have to enter your living space.

Perhaps the most attractive aspect of basement remodeling is the cost. Being buried underground reduces the need for exterior finish. The rough floors, walls, and ceiling are already in place and a finished roof covers everything. This means there's a lot less work that needs to be done. As a general rule of thumb, when a basement is constructed to the same level of finish as an addition, it can cost about 50 percent less.

top • Every bit of window area is precious in basement spaces, so find ways to squeeze in what you can. One effective technique is to follow the exterior grade by lengthening the windows as the grade drops.

above • French doors have their place inside a basement. Closed, this handsome pair of double doors acoustically separate the sitting area from the rest of the basement, yet maintains a visually open feeling. If you need privacy, look for doors with blinds between the glass, or simply add them on one side.

left • Delicious is the best way to describe this color composition. The dark plum of the closet acts as the visual center without overwhelming the space, whereas the contrast between the lighter shades of purple on the walls and ceiling sharply defines those different surfaces. The red pool table surface adds punch.

The Ups and Downs of Stairs

Most basement stairs are typically hidden behind a blank wall and accessed through a narrow, windowless door that may swing awkwardly into a hall or kitchen. This configuration effectively puts a roadblock between the first floor and the basement, making access difficult. Removing the full-height wall on the first floor and replacing it with either a half-wall or a balustrade creates an inviting entry and allows natural light from the first floor to flood the steps. It also can visually expand the first-floor space.

If the type of room planned for the basement—a playroom, for example—benefits from the physical separation that a first-floor wall provides, consider installing windows in the wall. Also think about replacing the solid door leading to the basement with one that has glass, preferably full-height. This not only blocks sound but also gives a more open feeling and allows some light to penetrate the stairs. If the basement stairs are closed off with walls at the basement level, open them up as well.

Current building codes require stairs to be constructed a minimum of 36 in. wide, which is really the minimum width for comfort when using the stairs as well as for moving furniture in and out of the space. Because many older homes have an even narrower stairway, opening them up might be a necessity to meet current codes.

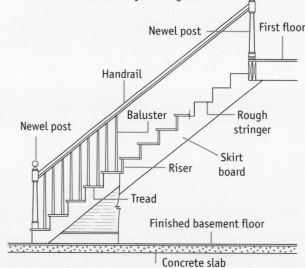

Stair Components

Stair components come in a variety of styles and finishes, so the choices may feel overwhelming. Take your cues from the other woodwork that is in your home and, of course, any existing stairs.

Newel post

First floor

Handrail

Baluster

Rough stringer

Newel post

Skirt board

Riser

Tread

Finished basement floor

Concrete slab

There are some circumstances that call for even more radical measures. Sometimes as the basement design develops it becomes clear that, in their current position, the stairs severely compromise the floor plan. Completely moving a set of stairs to a new location is difficult and costly, but it could very well mean the difference between a space that is used to its fullest potential and one that becomes nothing more than a beautiful storage room. Of course, the relocated stairs have to work with the first-floor plan, too.

First impressions are important and the stairs should set the tone for the entire basement. Nicely detailed handrails and balusters are important. The treads can be clear-finish hardwood with pine risers. If sound or footing is an issue, a high-quality stair runner can be installed. If your home has a chair rail or wainscoting, the stairs can be similarly detailed.

left · Have a little fun by giving a stair railing a custom look. Although these playful balusters may look intricate, they're not as complicated as they appear. Stock 1×1s and 2×2s were installed in an alternating pattern, and circle cutouts, which give the railing its custom look, were attached to both ends of the 1×1 balusters.

facing page · The simple but elegant guardrail at the top of this set of stairs opens up the basement to the kitchen and adjacent hall, bringing design consistency to the spaces and adding light to the below-grade level. The same natural-finished wood rail and painted square balusters are also used for the stair railing and echo the kitchen décor.

Stair Designs

Stair railings are often a prominent feature of a remodeled basement and present a great opportunity to introduce a little flair into your new lower-level rooms. Although the typical handrail and baluster arrangement is certainly adequate, unusual railing configurations can really make a statement.

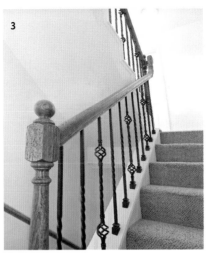

1. Sleek steel cables contrast with the warm wood treads and risers, yet are the perfect compliment to this modern flight of stairs. Their thin cross section make them visually unobtrusive and maximize a feeling of openness. 2. Stock materials can be used in creative ways. Here standard 2×2 balusters are installed in an interesting grid pattern. When venturing outside normal installation patterns, make sure the design meets building code requirements. 3. The combination of wooden handrails and forged steel balusters sets this railing apart from the everyday. Available in a wide array of styles and profiles, an almost endless number of patterns and designs can be created with steel balusters. 4. A relatively inexpensive way to make a stair railing is to build a half-wall. To protect the top of the wall, cap it with smoothly finished wood. The railing cap can be the same as the rest of the trim or, to create a contrasting element, finished differently.

Lighting the Way

Light is crucial to a well-designed basement room that's a pleasure to be in. Unfortunately, basements by their very nature are light-challenged because they're underground. Basements typically have very few, and very small, windows. Although "walkout" basements may have full-size windows, they don't let in adequate daylight for a truly habitable basement. Providing adequate artificial lighting in basements is a must.

Actually, basement lighting needs to be more than just adequate. Without the access to plentiful natural light that upper floors enjoy, much more time should be spent thinking about basement lighting than is typical for the rest of a home. Good lighting design requires a multidimensional approach. Sometimes referred to as "light layering," this technique combines two or more of the four types of lighting—ambient, task, accent, and decorative—to not only provide comfortable illumination levels but also add interest and character to a room. Lighting techniques can be hard to visualize in the abstract, so it's a good idea to see some actual examples of well-lit rooms and to visit lighting showrooms.

Moving Stairs

The stairs to the basement in this 1960s-era house were double trouble. Located about 5 ft. inside the front door, they were actually a hazard for people entering the home. In the basement the stairs ate up valuable living space and created an awkward traffic pattern. The only way to address both of these issues was to move the stairs.

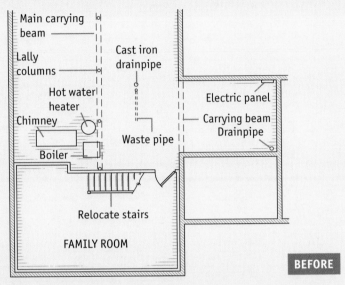

Main carrying beam
Lally columns
Cast iron drainpipe
Hot water heater
Chimney
Electric panel
Carrying beam
Drainpipe
Boiler
Waste pipe
Relocate stairs
FAMILY ROOM
BEFORE

The basement family room was narrow to begin with and the placement of the stairs made matters worse.

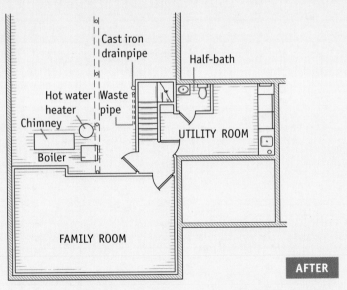

Cast iron drainpipe
Half-bath
Hot water heater
Waste pipe
Chimney
UTILITY ROOM
Boiler
FAMILY ROOM
AFTER

The now centrally located stairs make efficient use of the basement space. Without the stairs running through it, the family room is good size and in fact can double as a guest room. The washer and drier were moved to their own space, leaving plenty of room for the mechanical equipment and storage.

Some thought should also be given to light switches. Try to imagine walking through and living in the space. Locate the switches so that you can turn a light on when you enter and off if you leave through another door. In a bedroom, make sure that a least one light can be controlled without having to get out of bed. Choose a height off of the floor you feel comfortable with—42 in. to 48 in. to the center of the box is standard—and place all the switches at the same height. Finally, make sure switches are not located behind the door swing. Consider, too, the use of dimmers, which allow you to instantly change the mood of a room.

Of course, the best plan is not worth very much if it's not implemented, and when it comes to a lighting plan, that means an ample budget. Money spent on a sufficient number of quality lighting fixtures is not just an expense but an important investment.

above · This conversation grouping is softly lit by high-style ceiling-mounted fixtures. The opaque glass shades allow some light to shine directly downward, but direct much of the light to the ceiling, helping to create an intimate feeling.

facing page · Basement stairs can be more than just serviceable. Here, stainless steel cables replace balusters in this modern railing system, which results in a very open effect. With dramatic flair, the first floor is cut away in a graceful curve and the light-colored, wood-paneled walls and matching stair treads reflect the light that pours through the opening.

Rehabilitating a Bad Remodeling Job

This 1950s-era raised ranch was in need of some care, particularly the basement, which was suffering from severe neglect, a result of an early ill-conceived remodeling job. Low ceilings, cheap materials, and water problems combined to make the space virtually uninhabitable. The new owners, with the help of their builder, had a different vision, but it required some radical measures.

BEFORE

To create ample headroom, the old concrete floor was demolished and 60 yd. of dirt were hauled away. Before a new concrete floor was installed, waterproofing measures were taken to address the moisture problems caused by the high water table. To ensure a cozy, warm floor, the floor was insulated and radiant heating pipes were incorporated. And to create an all-in-one finished floor, the wet concrete was stamped and sealed to give it the look of slate.

Creating a physical and visual connection to the outside, an important part of any up-to-date remodeling project, was relatively easy to do. Two pairs of French doors, flanked by fixed panels and chosen to match the existing windows, were installed in a fully exposed exterior wall.

BEFORE

facing page · Aligning the new French doors underneath the existing windows restored a sense of order, whereas covering the exposed concrete with shingle siding integrated the basement with the rest of the house. The new flagstone patio adds outdoor living space, making the basement an even more attractive part of the home.

top · This light-filled exercise space not only has a great view but also easy access to the backyard.

Flooring

Floors take a lot of abuse, so they should be made of quality materials that can stand up to wear and tear. But floors can serve more than a strictly utilitarian purpose. Finish flooring has a big visual impact, and beautiful, eye-catching effects can be created by incorporating different types of flooring materials and installation patterns.

Contrary to popular belief, the range of flooring materials that can be used in basements is very broad. It is important to understand that installing a finish floor over a basement concrete slab does present some special challenges, chief among them moisture diffusion. Therefore, not every flooring material is right for every type of installation. However, if a particular material is matched with the appropriate installation method, basement flooring choices are almost the same as those for above-grade floors.

An important consideration when choosing the type of flooring and the installation method is how a floor feels underfoot. For example, a concrete slab is much less forgiving than above-grade floors, which are typically built with wooden joists and plywood, so the same material installed directly on a concrete slab will feel significantly stiffer. One of the goals in basement remodeling is to create a space that mimics the rest of the home as much as possible, so the flooring you choose should not only take that into consideration but also how the basement room—or rooms—will be used. A playroom will likely warrant a different flooring material than a home theater or guest bedroom.

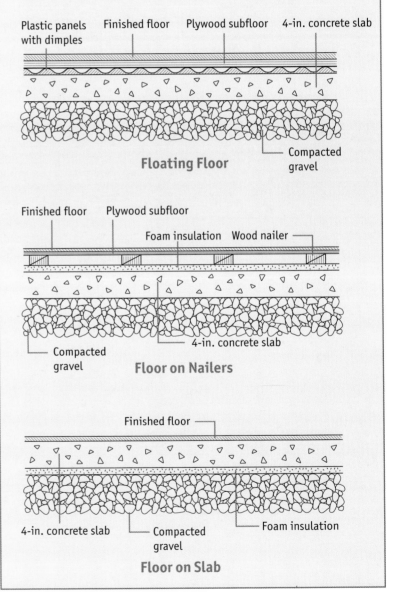

Finished-Floor Components

There are three methods of installing floors on a concrete slab. Some offer better warmth and more resilience underfoot than others. The installation approach depends on how smooth the concrete is and what kind of finished floor you want. Some floor assemblies are thicker than others and could impact the headroom in the finished space, so think about flooring early on in the design process.

Plastic panels with dimples Finished floor Plywood subfloor 4-in. concrete slab

Compacted gravel

Floating Floor

Finished floor Plywood subfloor Foam insulation Wood nailer

Compacted gravel 4-in. concrete slab

Floor on Nailers

Finished floor

4-in. concrete slab Compacted gravel Foam insulation

Floor on Slab

above · Good lighting doesn't have to be complex to be effective. Portable table and floor lamps provide flexibility not offered by hard-wired fixtures. They can be used to fill in darker areas and are perfect when placed near chairs and couches for reading.

left · An effective way to differentiate various areas within an open space is by using different flooring materials. Here, tile, which is impervious to spilled liquids, is used around the bar. Richly finished tongue-and-groove wood flooring adds style to the dining area and acts as a walkway separating the carpet from the tile.

facing page · Flooring can be used to unify spaces, making them feel larger and less busy. The low-pile carpet sweeps from the media center, through the dining area, and around to and under the French doors that close off a home office. The same carpet is used on the stairs, making them appear to be an extension of the floor.

Walls and Ceilings

Basement remodeling has gotten a bad rap because of what many people visualize when they think "finished basement": knotty pine paneling and a drop ceiling with institutional-looking ceiling tiles. Although those materials are still used, they are no longer the norm. In fact, remodeled basements are as beautiful and luxurious as any other room in the home.

WALLS

Once again, when it comes to wall finishes, treat basement walls the same as any other walls in a home. As with floors, basement walls may be constructed differently than above-ground walls, but the choice of materials is wide open. In fact, because a basement slab can support a lot more weight than a wood-framed floor, heavy materials—such as stone and glass block—can often be used without the need for additional structural support.

Several things should be considered before choosing the type of wall material and the color of the finish. The first is light. Although creating a bright basement by introducing as much artificial and natural light as possible is of prime importance, light-colored paint, wallpaper, and wood finishes that reflect light enhance a room's brightness. Dark colors absorb light, so they should be used sparingly. Smooth and shiny materials will also help reflect light. Rough-wood unfinished paneling, for example, will not reflect as much light as wood that has been sanded smooth and finished with a low-gloss urethane. Smooth finishes are also much friendlier to the touch, so they are a good option if you anticipate lots of kids and adults moving around the space and leaning up against the walls.

Next is height. Most basements are vertically challenged, but there are a number of visual tricks that can be used to make a basement feel higher. Wallpaper with a vertical pattern and wood paneling that's installed vertically will tend to "lift" the ceiling. Introducing narrow elements, such as bookcases, accentuates the vertical sense. Creating other visual tricks with paint—such as a faux tray ceiling—is another option.

left • This neutral color scheme is sophisticated and clean, letting the details shine: granite countertop, wide baseboard trim and panel detailing around the bar, pendant lights, and artwork. With no natural light in this space, the simplicity keeps the room feeling light and airy.

below • Increasing the thickness of the walls surrounding this doorway created enough depth for two built-in bookcases. Lifting the bottom shelf up off of the floor aligns it with the baseboard and makes room for a heating grill.

facing page • One wall of this basement room is light, the other darker. The contrast in color gives more depth to the space and creates a thoughtful, sophisticated look.

Wall Surfaces

When thinking about your basement's finished wall surfaces keep an open mind and an eye toward the type of atmosphere you're trying to create. Whether neutral painted walls, highly detailed surfaces, or fanciful creations, choose the style that fits the space and its use, suits your taste, and is within your budget.

TILE

STONE

DRYWALL
$

- Can be painted or covered with wallpaper
- Susceptible to nicks and gouges
- Relatively easy to patch
- Moisture-resistant types should be used in moist areas

WOOD AND WOOD LOOK-ALIKES
$–$$

- A wide variety of solid wood species and engineered materials are available
- Wood can be painted; stains and clear finishes highlight wood's natural beauty
- More durable than drywall but harder to patch
- Solid wood expands and contracts with changes in moisture levels

TILE AND STONE
$$–$$$

- Extremely durable
- Impervious to water; can be used for tub surrounds and shower walls
- Numerous styles, colors, and finishes to choose from
- May be difficult to repair, depending on the type of installation

FIBERGLASS PANELS
$

- Easy to install
- Panels can be replaced
- Absorbs sound
- Fabric-covered panels are soft and give when touched

WALLPAPER

TONGUE-AND-GROOVE BOARDS

WOOD PANELING

CEILINGS

The great debate about basement ceilings is between hung ceilings and drywall ceilings. One of the most frequent arguments made in favor of hung ceilings is access. After all, a finished ceiling covers up myriad pipes and wires, and if a sink or toilet leaks or a pipe breaks a hung ceiling provides easy access to do the necessary repairs. But there are a lot of pipes and wires in the ceilings of one-story houses, and sinks and toilets in two-story homes—but no hung ceilings. Why should the basement be treated any differently? It doesn't have to be. An access panel can be installed in a drywall ceiling, and, if necessary, it's relatively easy to cut out and patch dry wall.

Ease of installation and less mess are other advantages of a hung ceiling. Ceiling tiles come packed in a box and cut neatly with a utility knife. The metal frame gridwork that holds the tiles is snipped with shears. The workers are in and out in a day or two. With a drywall ceiling, the mess of cutting, sawing, and sanding drywall needs to be considered—the dust just seems to get everywhere. As with wall finish, the ceiling finish creates a particular look and feel in the room, so the desired look more than anything should be the primary reason behind using one type over another.

One distinct advantage a drywall ceiling has over a hung ceiling is height. A hung ceiling must be installed about 3 in. to 4 in. below the rough ceiling. This is a problem in most basements, where every inch of height matters. Depending on the type of installation, drywall reduces headroom by only an inch or two.

Cost, of course, is part of the mix. Budget may dictate that you use a hung ceiling, because this type of ceiling material tends to be less expensive than drywall, especially if there are a lot of pipes and obstructions to box in. When choosing a hung ceiling, however, 2-ft. by 2-ft. tiles with an edge reveal are a more appropriate scale and style than 2-ft. by 4-ft. tiles. If the grid is the same color as the tile, the ceiling won't stand out too much.

above · Detailed to match the base of the bar and the custom wine storage rack that surrounds the mirror, the coffered ceiling helps to create a sense of place for this small basement bar. Tiny recessed lights installed in the false beams further define the space.

left · Richly detailed woodwork on the ceiling that echoes the sophisticated yet comfortable furnishings helps to define the seating area while blending in smoothly with the rest of this adult getaway.

Ceiling Materials

Without a doubt, installing a finished ceiling is more of a challenge in basements than in most other spaces in a house. The challenges, however, can result in some very creative solutions that add character to a room.

HUNG CEILING TILES
$

- Easy to install
- Installation doesn't make much mess
- Wide range of textures
- Absorbs sound better than other materials
- Provides easy access to pipes
- Individual tiles are easy to replace
- Low-cost materials can look cheap

DRYWALL
$$

- Readily available
- Can be installed around unusual shapes
- Easy to paint and patch
- Makes a room's finish look seamless

WOOD
$$$

- Naturally beautiful
- Time-consuming to install
- Can be used as accents or to enclose rough beams
- Darker woods will not reflect light as well as other finishes

TIN
$$$

- Many styles and patterns to choose from
- May reflect sound more than other materials
- Effective for creating ceiling accents

CEILING TILES

DRYWALL

TIN

Adding Windows

When it comes to basements, windows present a particularly vexing problem. A basement that is just, well, a basement doesn't have much need for windows. Standard basement windows are very few and very small—about 30 in. long and 18 in. high—and are sized to meet basement building code requirements. But if a basement is to be transformed into viable living space those windows just won't do. There has to be more of them, and they have to be bigger. Larger windows may also be required by code. Installing windows in a basement may seem like a formidable task, but it's not as difficult as it might appear.

Foundations can be cut relatively easily with the proper tools, and the earth around them can be moved. Fortunately, many basements are not completely buried. The ground often slopes away on one or more sides, exposing a portion, or all, of the foundation. If the long side of the house is exposed, that wall can virtually be filled with windows. This makes window installation a breeze. The challenge is a bit greater for a house with the narrow end wall exposed.

One of the goals of installing windows is to allow light to penetrate as far as possible into a basement. That's difficult when windows are only placed in the end wall. However, the ground on one or both adjacent sides can be dug away to create a steeper slope, or terraced with retaining walls. Although they may be shorter, this allows windows to be installed along the long side of the house.

If a house is completely surrounded on all sides there may be only one available option: window wells. But not the small, old-fashioned basement window wells. A livable basement needs window wells that are as large and deep as possible. If a window array is long, the wells can be custom built. Premade window wells are also available that are constructed from rot-resistant materials such as polyethylene.

It's no accident that this basement space enjoys a generous amount of light. First, the stairs are open for more than half their length, allowing the light from the large windows on the landing to cascade down the steps. More intriguing, however, is how the upper portion of the stairs is pulled away from the outside wall, permitting the installation of a wide floor-to-ceiling window.

Types of Windows

Ordinarily when remodeling you'd choose new windows to match the existing—the same type, style, and general size. However, given the restrictions that basements often present, that may not be possible. When this happens, try to find a unit that fits best with the design of your home and yet still works in the basement.

DOUBLE-HUNG
$$

- Traditional style
- Top and bottom sashes can be opened independently
- Wide range of sizes
- Shorter units may not qualify for emergency egress

CASEMENT
$$

- Fairly modern look
- Window cranks out from side or middle
- Wide range of sizes
- Many sizes qualify for emergency egress
- Seal tighter than double-hung units
- Open windows may present an outdoor hazard

AWNING
$

- Limited sizes
- Generally don't qualify for emergency egress
- Can be stacked under fixed units to provide ventilation

SLIDING
$$

- Open horizontally
- Wide range of sizes
- Have the look of casement windows but don't project outside

FIXED
$–$$

- Don't open
- Available in custom shapes and sizes
- Generally cost less than other types of windows

DOUBLE-HUNG

CASEMENT

AWNING

SLIDING

An Open and Shut Case for Doors

Doors have a dual personality. They can open things up or shut them out. Although doors are certainly necessary in a basement remodel, here's a situation where less may be more. As mentioned earlier, a hallmark of a successful basement design is a generally open floor plan where rooms and spaces are defined by, among other things, half-walls and dividers. This makes the rooms appear larger and lets light flow from space to space. Fewer walls mean fewer doors.

Careful consideration should be given to the types of doors that are used in an up-to-date basement remodel. Solid doors are a must in some rooms—bathrooms and bedrooms, for example. But to create and maintain an open feeling, doors with glass in them should be used wherever possible. French doors not only increase sight lines and light penetration; they also add a stylish touch.

There may be situations that call for specialty doors. A fire-rated door may be required to separate the space that contains the heating equipment. Someone who wants peace and quiet will appreciate a heavy door that's sealed with gaskets on all four edges. If a standard door doesn't work, custom doors can be built to hide service panels, close off odd-shaped storage areas, or blend with a chosen décor.

Swinging doors can be in the way when they are open. This can be particularly annoying in a basement, where doors are likely to be left open for long stretches of time. Sliding doors hung on tracks or pocket doors that slip into the wall are great space-savers, especially if they are used instead of double French doors. Because the cracks around these types of doors are hard to seal, they may not be the best choice to block sound.

top • Not only are French doors a beautiful addition to a walk-out basement, but they also serve two practical functions. They create the all-important physical connection with the outside, and they let the outdoors—in the form of views and light—inside.

above • This four-panel swinging door is incorporated into the playful garden scene that's created by the murals. With door and trim painted the same color as the walls, the door almost disappears, creating the illusion of a hole in the fence.

Types of Doors

A range of door styles are available to fit every taste and budget. Be sure to choose a type that blends with the décor and is compatible with how it's going to be used. And be sure to buy the best-quality door you can afford.

FLUSH DOORS—HOLLOW AND SOLID CORE
$ hollow core; $$ solid core

- Smooth surface goes well with more modern styles
- Lauan veneers are typically painted, birch veneers are stained or clear finished
- Hollow-core doors feel cheap, can only be cut down a small amount, and don't provide much sound isolation
- Solid-core doors are heavy, can be trimmed to shorter size, and provide better sound isolation than hollow-core doors
- Don't swell or shrink

MOLDED DOORS—HOLLOW AND SOLID CORE
$ hollow core; $$ solid core

- Made from compressed wood fibers
- Mimic panel doors
- Solid-core doors resist dings and dents
- Come preprimed, ready for painting
- Panel styles may be limited

SOLID WOOD PANEL DOORS
$$$

- Available in hardwoods or softwoods
- Showcase natural beauty of wood when clear finished or stained
- Swell and shrink with changes in humidity
- Wide range of panel styles

LOUVER DOORS
$$

- Slats allow ventilation through door
- Not appropriate where privacy or sound isolation required
- Available in full louver or louver-and-panel style

FRENCH DOORS
$$$

- Made in exterior and interior versions
- Available with full-length, one-piece glass; true or simulated divided lights; frosted or stained glass
- Will not block as much noise as solid-type doors since glass transmits more sound

STEEL DOORS
$

- Primarily used as exterior doors
- Come preprimed, ready to paint
- May rust or dent
- Provide better thermal insulation than solid wood doors

FIBERGLASS DOORS—SMOOTH AND WOOD TEXTURED
$$–$$$

- Primarily used as exterior doors
- Will not rust or dent
- Provide better thermal insulation than solid wood doors
- Smooth-surface doors can be painted
- Textured-surface types can cost as much as solid wood doors

PANEL

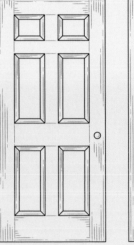

LOUVER

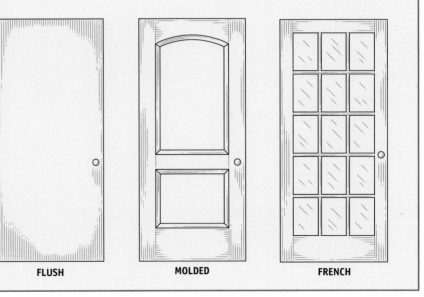

FLUSH   MOLDED   FRENCH

From Storage Room to Family Room

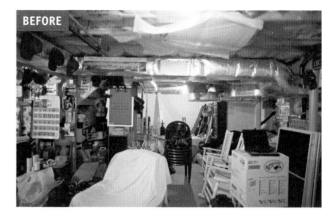

BEFORE

Before it was transformed into a neat, clean, multiuse family room, this basement was nothing but 1,200 sq. ft. of storage. Ducts and pipes crisscrossed the ceiling, installed well below the joists, and insulation was hanging down from between the joists. Six seemingly randomly placed Lally columns broke up the space. In spite of these challenges, the homeowners had big plans for this space.

They envisioned a TV area, small home gym, kitchenette, guest bedroom, full bath with a steam shower, wine closet, and space for a pool table, and they got their wish. Through clever planning, all but two of the Lally columns were hidden, incorporated into the newly constructed walls. This allowed the space to be broken into task-related areas rather than based on where the support structures were placed. To meet the building codes, egress windows with window wells were added in the guest room and in the TV area.

Because storage was still needed by the homeowners, they constructed a large walk-in storage area, equipped with built-in shelves.

above · The once cluttered basement adds valuable living space to the home. The unruly ducts have been moved and hidden in soffits, which help to define the spaces. The light-colored walls and floors add to the open feeling.

facing page · This basement turned family room utilizes an L-shaped floor plan to create several areas: a place to watch television, a snack and drink center, and a game area. The two exposed posts, which might otherwise have been intrusive, help define the game area, and small shelves built around them make the perfect place to set a drink while you line up that next shot.

PLANNING

Creating that perfect basement is work, especially if your dreams call for more than one type of room. But it can be fun, too. Proper planning will keep

YOUR FINISHED

the process from getting too chaotic and help ensure that your finished basement meets—or exceeds—your expectations.

BASEMENT

Make a Wish List

One of the most important and enjoyable aspects of planning a finished basement (or any remodeling project for that matter) is dreaming about the possibilities. So go ahead, dream big. Look at magazines, talk to friends, hold brainstorming sessions with your family, search everywhere for ideas that you might want to include in your remodeled basement. As you clip pictures and gather literature, jot down notes to help you remember what you like when you go back through them weeks or maybe months down the road. For now don't worry about budget—that will make an appearance all too soon.

At some point you'll have to reluctantly call a halt to all this daydreaming and reenter reality. As you do, take a hard look at what kind of needs and activities your remodeled basement should fulfill. A place for the family to gather? Or a spot for that treadmill that's in the living room? How about somewhere to get away from it all? Also, try to see into the future. Families grow and shrink, and needs are constantly changing. Will your basement be able to keep up?

In addition to making a clip file, create a wish list of everything you might possibly want. Ask each family member to do the same. Divide the lists into two columns: one for types of spaces, the other for kinds of things. Also, establish a "sequence of surrender," prioritizing your list from the top down, from most to least important. That way when budget constraints shorten your lists, it will be from the bottom up.

top • There's no doubt that billiards takes center stage in this finished basement that was decorated to resemble a neighborhood pub. Even the bar stools play their part, with striped fabric resembling the striping of the pool balls.

right • Although the wall adjacent to the short flight of steps has been removed, the wall along the hallway remains, creating privacy for the seating group positioned in the corner of the room. The lower portion of the exterior walls is concrete and thicker than the wood-frame walls built on top of them. The difference in thickness forms a perfectly sized display shelf.

facing page • An eclectic collection of furniture and furnishings can work together to create a comfortable ensemble. Here, the varying styles are tied together by their similar earth tones.

Assembling Your Team

From the initial planning and design stages through to the finished project, converting a basement into prime living space is a complicated task that requires the help of building professionals. Here are some of the people who might be involved:

• **An architect, building designer, and interior designer** can all help with the design of your project. A licensed architect is highly educated, trained, and familiar with all aspects of design and construction. Choose an architect who specializes in residential design. Building designers and interior designers usually have some amount of formal training or may belong to a professional organization that requires a minimum level of expertise. All qualified designers can prepare the plans and specifications you'll need to gather prices for your project. Architects and designers typically work by the hour or charge their fee as a percentage of the cost of construction. Some states may mandate the services of a licensed architect.

• **A licensed structural engineer** may be required if your plans call for removing or relocating a post, beam, or carrying wall. Input from an engineer in the early planning stages can be very helpful, steering you away from potentially expensive ideas or giving you the go-ahead for others.

• **A general contractor** (also called a GC and often referred to as a builder) prepares a complete price, or estimate, for the entire scope of the work and oversees the construction of your project. A general contractor may have employees who perform some of the work—typically the rough framing and finish carpentry. However, the GC gathers prices from, and retains the services of, subcontractors, such as electricians, plumbers, drywall installers, and painters, who perform the bulk of the work. The GC schedules the work, coordinates the subs, and is ultimately responsible for the quality of the job.

• **A construction manager** is sometimes hired by a homeowner on larger jobs to act as the owner's agent and verify that the project is being constructed according to the plans and specifications. Architects and designers often offer construction management services, separate from their design services. Construction management fees are usually in the range of 10 to 15 percent of the cost of the project.

Understanding Basement Construction

It may not be tops on your list of "things I've always wanted to learn about," but a basic understanding of basement construction is important. This knowledge gives you a better sense of the special design challenges that basements present. Plus, when you talk with the building professionals who will help to turn your dreams into reality, you won't feel like they're conversing in a foreign language.

Basement construction is relatively simple and consists of three major components: floor, foundation walls, and ceiling. In a completely unfinished basement the structure is exposed and easy to see. If you're planning to redo a previously finished basement some of the existing finish material will have to be removed to reveal the structural elements.

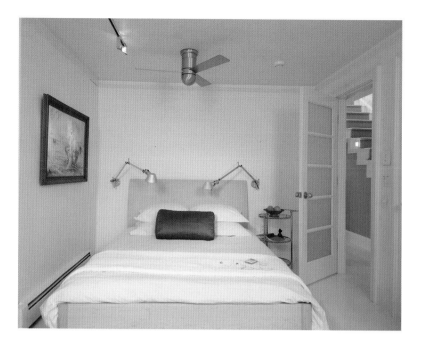

ROUGH FLOORS

A cursory inspection of your basement floor will tell you whether it is dirt, concrete, or a combination of the two. A dirt floor can be easily prepped for a new smooth concrete slab floor, over which just about any kind of finish floor can be installed. Plus, if you need or want more headroom, it's much easier to remove dirt than to break up and haul away concrete.

Old concrete floors need to be carefully assessed. They may be cracked, broken, or even buckled. It's possible to repair such a floor, but if it is severely damaged the best alternative may be to remove the entire floor and pour a new one. In homes built later than 1980, concrete floors tend to be more highly finished and have relatively smooth surfaces. They may have been constructed with wire mesh, fiberglass reinforcing, or control joints to help reduce cracking, and it may be possible to install finished floors right over them.

above • **This small guest room located off the side of the basement stairs is just large enough to accommodate a twin bed. Reading lights mounted to the headboard makes efficient use of space, and positioning the head of the bed behind the door swing creates more privacy.**

left • **Pool tables are a common finished basement fixture, but they don't have to be hidden in a dark corner. Wide-open spaces allow plenty of room for those otherwise cramped shots along the side rails, and light-colored surfaces in the room eliminate a gloomy atmosphere.**

facing page • **The section of low ceiling in this room actually makes the rest of the room feel taller. The trick is to emphasize the height difference by keeping the low space dark and brightly lighting the other space.**

Basement Structure

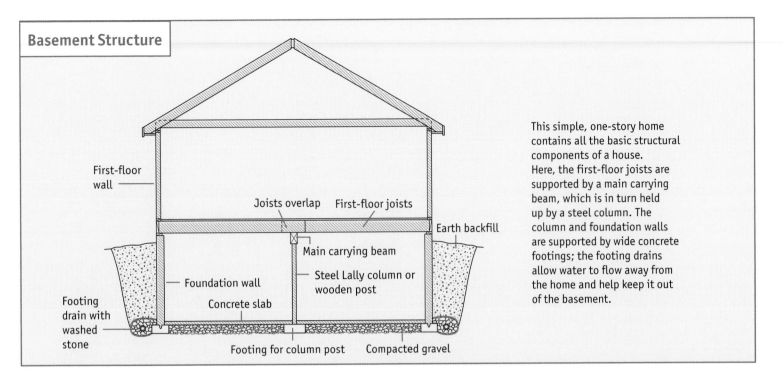

First-floor wall

Joists overlap   First-floor joists

Earth backfill

Main carrying beam

Foundation wall

Steel Lally column or wooden post

Concrete slab

Footing drain with washed stone

Footing for column post   Compacted gravel

This simple, one-story home contains all the basic structural components of a house. Here, the first-floor joists are supported by a main carrying beam, which is in turn held up by a steel column. The column and foundation walls are supported by wide concrete footings; the footing drains allow water to flow away from the home and help keep it out of the basement.

Opening Up the Stairs

It's common for basement stairs to run the same direction as the first-floor joists—perpendicular to the length of the house. Positioned this way they usually work well with the first-floor plan. They are also much easier to install because the floor joists don't have to be cut. However, one problem with this approach is that the bottom of the stairs often ends up very close to the outside wall. This not only creates a physical bottleneck but also a visual obstruction.

Although it's possible to move the stairs to solve these problems, that's a costly proposition and could have a negative impact on the first-floor plan. A much less expensive and easier solution is to open the stairs up at the bottom by removing as much of the sidewalls as possible and replacing them with a handrail. Choosing a railing style that is delicately scaled and finished with light colors will allow the railing to blend into the surroundings and maximize the open feeling. A railing that goes over the top of the end post also feels less obtrusive.

above · Replacing the wall on both sides with handrails makes the bottom of these stairs feel wide open. The rounded volutes above the last tread add style and make turning the corner feel smoother.

left · A swinging French door at the top of the stairs keeps noise from the basement out of the main level but allows light to filter down. Widening the bottom of the stairs and leaving them open to the basement helps the lower level feel more spacious.

above · These adjustable shelves are intended more for displaying artwork and knickknacks than holding books. Painted white and left uncluttered, they help to focus attention on the stone fireplace.

top left · Positioned off the side, along a section of wall, this compact work station combines business with style. Placing the bookshelf on top of the desk is an efficient use of a small space.

bottom left · Given a quick look, this wall seems to hold a random display of prints, but a closer inspection reveals their commonality. This careful arrangement even integrates the wall sconces, making them part of the overall composition, helping to give this otherwise orphaned space presence.

FOUNDATION WALLS

A quick look at the foundation walls tells you what type you have. If your home was constructed before 1900 it's likely that the foundation is made of stone. Concrete block and cast-in-place concrete foundations were introduced in the early 1900s. Block foundations were initially more popular because they were easier and cheaper to build. Today, however, both types are used throughout the country and make up the majority of modern foundations.

Although their use is not widespread, there are several other types of foundations, including precast concrete panels, insulating-foam concrete forms that remain in place after the concrete is poured, and all-wood foundations built with pressure-treated lumber and plywood.

above · Things don't always have to be covered up to be hidden. Sporting a coat of white paint, the low-hanging pipes and ductwork in this shower area almost seem to disappear. Although they don't seem out of place in this informal room, the nicely detailed floor helps to draw attention away from them.

right · Cleverly tucked into a jog in the basement wall, this built-in does double duty— daytime couch and nighttime bed. Supportive cushions help to make it more functional as a couch, and the swing-arm lamp provides much needed light in the corner.

facing page · Hollow porch columns, either made of wood or polymer materials, can be used to encase unsightly steel Lallys. They are available in a wide range of styles to blend with most any décor. This elegant, slightly tapered column is completely in tune with its surroundings.

CEILINGS

The basement ceiling is formed by the home's first-floor joists. They span from one side of the foundation to the other. The joists are usually supported near midspan by a carrying beam, which is in turn held up by steel posts called Lally columns. Houses built in the last decade or so might feature I-joists, which can often span a basement without the need of supporting beams and columns.

One of the most important structural considerations when thinking about remodeling or converting a basement to living space is ceiling height. For a room to feel comfortable the ceiling height must be adequate. Basements rarely have ceilings that are as high as the upper levels, which are typically 8 ft. or more. Ceiling height is also governed by buildings codes. So, if your ceiling seems unusually low, you should check with the building inspector to find out if it meets code requirements. If it doesn't, you should find out if it's feasible to dig the floor out enough to come into compliance.

Dealing with Obstructions

Dealing with structural obstructions, like beams and columns, is a way of life when remodeling a basement. There's just no way around it. Or is there? All it takes is some clever thinking and a little elbow grease to create any number of inventive solutions to the problems caused by structural obstacles.

facing page • Sometimes the best way to address an obstruction is to emphasize it. The effect of the massive fluted column supporting the simple rectangular beam is striking.

below • This relatively deep beam creates the edge of this modest seating group. It is crisply wrapped in drywall, which reduces its visual impact; painted the same color as the ceiling, it almost disappears.

Design Tricks to Address Basement Shortcomings

Basements present a number of design challenges. Here are some tricks you can use to help you deal with them effectively.

Make spaces feel taller by:

• Using 6 ft. 6 in. doors instead of standard 6 ft. 8 in. doors.

• Breaking very long spaces up with half-walls or dividers.

• Using narrower trim on doors and for baseboards in small, low spaces.

• Keeping hallways less than 42 in. wide.

• Using vertical elements, such as narrow bookshelves, paneling, and patterned wallpaper.

• Hanging pictures a bit lower than usual.

• Painting the ceiling and the walls the same color.

Make spaces feel larger by:

• Reducing the number of full-height walls to create an open floor plan.

• Installing doors with glass in them.

• Using light-colored paints, flooring, and furnishings.

• Installing large or even full-wall mirrors.

• Using angled and curved walls where possible.

• Bumping out short sections of walls.

Maximize the space by:

• Making use of odd-shaped spaces, such as under the stairs.

• Hiding mechanical equipment in multipurpose built-ins, like benches.

• Recessing shelves into walls.

• Turning full or half-walls into shelves or bookcases.

Electric, phone, and cable TV wires that are installed in holes drilled through the center of the floor joists don't present much of a problem. It's another matter when they are stapled to the bottom of the joists. Although hung ceilings are installed below wires and avoid them altogether, installing drywall ceilings takes a little more work. Furring strips—typically ¾ in. thick—screwed to the joists create a space for the wires between the joists and the finished drywall.

Pipes—heating pipes from hot water boilers, hot and cold domestic water pipes, and drainpipes—are more difficult to deal with. Although they are sometimes installed above the bottom of the joists, more often they are secured to the bottom. Some drainpipes, for example, may run along an outside wall or drop down in the middle of a basement and exit under the slab. Moving a lot of pipes can be a budget buster and should be avoided unless absolutely necessary. Again, furring strips can be used to create a space between the pipes and the ceiling material, but because pipes are typically ½ in. to 1 in. in diameter, regular furring strips often won't work. Instead, 2-in. by 3-in. studs installed flat will provide enough space for most pipes. Walls can also be positioned to hide drainpipes.

WIRES, PIPES, AND DUCTWORK

Look up at a typical basement ceiling and you'll find a maze of wires, pipes, and ductwork. Some pose larger issues than others.

Ductwork delivers warm air from furnaces and/or cool air from air conditioners. The main trunks can be quite large—1 ft. deep and 2 ft. wide is common—and they are always installed below the joists. Smaller branch ducts deliver the air to the individual rooms. They may be below or between the joists. Moving ductwork can also be quite expensive, particularly if the system has to be redesigned. However, ductwork can be very intrusive and sometimes there's no other solution but to relocate it.

CARRYING BEAMS

Almost every basement has at least one large carrying beam. These beams typically run the length of the house and support the floor joists. Although some are built flush with the bottom of the joists, the vast majority are placed underneath them. In a typical basement these beams are less than 7 ft. from the floor and can be visually intrusive. This problem is magnified if your basement ceiling is lower than standard or there is more than one beam. There are ways, however, to duck this problem.

One way to deal with low-hanging beams is to incorporate them into the floor plan. Wherever possible, align walls underneath beams. In an open plan, use beams to visually separate one space from another. Locate built-ins such as half-walls, bookcases, and counters below beams. If your basement contains several beams, or if a beam runs right through the middle of a room, there's a more radical option: Turn it into a flush beam. The bottom of a flush beam is level with the bottom of the floor joists, and when the finished ceiling is installed the beam disappears.

top · Located at floor level, these child-height shelves make accessing and storing toys easy. The extra depth provides room for larger items that may be hard to store on standard-size shelves.

above · For architectural interest, this partial wall, which hides a Lally column, is punctuated with a rectangular opening. The top of the opening is capped with wood that can serve as a display shelf.

facing page · Ducts are often installed next to the main carrying beam, which makes concealing both the duct and the beam much easier. One large soffit can enclose them.

POSTS AND COLUMNS

Wherever there are beams, there are also posts. These two have an interesting relationship: Small beams need more posts, whereas larger beams require fewer posts. Older homes may have wooden 6-in. by 6-in. or 8-in. by 8-in. posts. Hollow steel poles called Lally columns—which are usually filled with concrete—are found in newer homes. If you're lucky, your basement has one simple row of columns lined up neatly under a main carrying beam. However, many basements are a maze of columns, and as with other obstructions, there are several ways to deal with unwanted columns.

As with beams, one effective approach to dealing with columns is to incorporate them into the floor plan. They can be hidden inside walls or anchor the ends of a half-wall. They can be dressed up and made a focal point. Sometimes, if a column is not too intrusive, the simplest approach is to camouflage it with a coat of paint and just live with it. However, columns that drastically disrupt the flow of a plan or pop up right in the middle of a space might have to be removed. All columns can support a significant amount of weight, though, so a structural engineer should be consulted before removing a column or any other structural member.

MECHANICAL EQUIPMENT

When your basement is remodeled the long-time residents—mechanical equipment such as warm air furnaces, hot water boilers, and water heaters—that once had the run of the place will have to share the space. They're not very accommodating. They are large, heavy, attached to pipes and ducts, and not easy to move. As a general rule, it's best to design around them. But there are exceptions to every rule. If your equipment is old or in need of replacement and its present location really puts a crimp in your remodeling plans, it might be worth moving it. If you go this route, consider direct-vent equipment, which doesn't require a chimney and ultimately opens up additional living space.

DETAILS THAT WORK

Camouflaging a Lally Column

The least expensive way to deal with Lally columns is to leave them where they are and just paint them. Here, the Lally column becomes part of the landscape as a climbing vine wraps around it.

above · At first glance this Lally column, which has been trimmed out to match the surrounding woodwork, would seem to be in the way. But it actually helps to direct the traffic flow by defining the travel space that's adjacent to, and goes around, the curved stairs.

facing page · The small footprint of these custom-made steel columns makes them feel less in the way, even though they're right in the center of the family room space. The wood detail at the top adds a contemporary touch and acknowledges the rest of the woodwork in the room.

Waterproofing Your Basement

We've all been in basements where we were assaulted by the smell of mildew, noticed that everything felt damp, and perhaps even encountered standing water. Up-to-date building materials and modern construction techniques can make this a thing of the past and mean a remodeled basement can be every bit as comfortable as the other spaces in your house.

facing page • Moisture issues typically associated with above-grade bathrooms are exacerbated in basement bathrooms. In addition to using materials that are waterproof and moisture resistant, like tile, it is extremely important to install a powerful fan that's capable of quickly exhausting the excess moisture created by showering.

below • The tall center unit breaks up a long bank of cabinets and shifts the emphasis from the horizontal to the vertical. The vertical feeling is accentuated by the narrow cabinet doors.

MOISTURE

Moisture enters basements in two forms: liquid water that flows on the surface or underground and water vapor. If the ground around a basement does not permit water to drain away easily, it can be forced into the basement through cracks in the walls or the joint between the foundation wall and footing. If the pressure is great enough water can actually be pushed right through the concrete walls and floors. Many foundation coating and waterproofing techniques won't prevent this type of leaking.

Water vapor migrates through concrete walls and floors and also enters basements through the gaps around windows and doors. Once inside, the vapor can condense out as liquid water on the cooler basement surfaces. The walls and floors of an unfinished basement may not show signs of water vapor because as the vapor moves through them it evaporates into the air, but it's there. Sealing water vapor behind finished walls and floors can trap it and allow it to condense.

The majority of basements leaks can be traced to surface water and are relatively easy to fix. This can include changing the grade around the foundation so it slopes away from the house, adding gutters to solve the problem of water running off the roof, and adding downspouts and leaders to carry water away from the foundation.

Breathe Deep

There are two health-related issues that need to be addressed to give your basement a clean bill of health: radon gas and indoor pollutants.

Radon gas is colorless, odorless, and tasteless and can cause lung cancer. Radon comes from the natural breakdown of uranium that's found in some soils, rocks, and water. The gas then diffuses into the air and gets into homes through gaps and cracks in the foundation walls and floors.

Before beginning a basement remodeling project, you should test your basement to determine if radon is present, and if so, at what levels. There are two types of tests—short term and long term. Because radon levels can vary from season to season it's more accurate to do a long-term test—more than 90 days.

If radon is present in your basement, you'll want to have all cracks, joints, and gaps sealed, then have an exhaust fan installed that vents to the outside to remove the radon gas that still enters the space. It's a good idea to hire a contractor who's trained in radon mitigation to design and install the right type of system.

In addition to radon gas, there are a number of other indoor air pollutants. Gases and chemicals produced or emitted from heating equipment, building materials and furnishings, and products used for household cleaning, personal care, and hobbies can build up in homes to unhealthy levels. Some sources, such as building materials, release pollutants on a more or less constant basis, whereas others, such as cleaning solvents, release pollutants only when used or if they're not stored properly.

Although it's virtually impossible to remove all the source of indoor pollution from the typical home, making sure that heating equipment is functioning properly, choosing furniture made without materials and glues that outgas harmful chemicals, and using natural cleaning products can significantly reduce pollution levels. To remove those pollutants that are released, it's important to install a properly designed ventilation system. For areas such as a workbench, consider installing an additional high-volume exhaust fan.

Green Building

Concern for the environment has never been greater. By using some of the green building materials and techniques listed here you can lessen the environmental impact of your basement remodeling project.

• Use wood—both flooring and lumber—that is certified as sustainably grown to promote long-term availability and health of forests. Another option is cork flooring, which is harvested from the cork oak tree and actually prolongs the life of the tree.

• Fabrics and products made from natural fibers and materials reduce the use of chemicals. Hemp grows quickly, and chemicals are not used when it's processed. Organically grown cotton is grown without chemicals. Tencel® fabrics, made from cellulose fiber and flax, linen products made from the flax plant, and wool rugs instead of synthetics are other options. Linoleum, a flooring product made from linseed oil, rosin, wood, and cork powder, is considered a green alternative to vinyl flooring.

• Reduce the levels of volatile organic compounds (VOCs). Use low-VOC or latex paints, and buy solid wood furniture or furniture made with composite materials that don't use glues and additives with VOCs.

• Use materials that have at least some recycled content and reclaimed materials to reduce the amount of waste that's hauled to landfills. Some carpet manufacturers only produce carpet that is made from 100-percent recycled material, and some brands of resilient flooring and acoustic ceiling tiles are made with recycled materials. Consider reclaimed flooring and paneling salvaged from old factory and mill buildings.

facing page · To underscore the hunting lodge theme established by the custom pool table and antler chandelier, the Lally column supporting the main wood carrying beam was replaced with a peeled log. Heavy wood trim at the top of the wall also adds to the effect.

right · A simple set of built-in drawers captures the unused space beneath the stairs. More intriguing, perhaps, is the base of this column. The base was left oversized to create a little storage cabinet, which is accessed through a small paneled door.

Your basement might have a sump pump, which would have been installed when the home was built to deal with water leakage caused by a high water table. You'll obviously need to accommodate the sump pump in your design, and you might also want to consider installing an alarm or backup power source in case of a power failure or malfunction. If your basement doesn't have a sump pump the only available option is to install an interior perimeter drain in the concrete floor, so you'll want to consult a contractor who specializes in basement waterproofing.

In spite of the best waterproofing techniques, water vapor will find its way into your basement. Walls and floors should be constructed with moisture-resistant materials that either allow vapor to pass through them or are installed in a manner that allows moisture to escape. Although moisture can be removed from the basement through open windows or exhaust fans, when humidity levels are high, such as during the summer months, a dehumidifier or air conditioner will be needed to keep your basement at a healthy moisture level.

Moving into the Design Phase

With a solid understanding of the issues that influence basement planning, you're now ready for a more enjoyable task: creating a working design for your finished space. Whether you hire an architect or builder or even take a crack at coming up with a design on your own, putting everything down on paper is important. This will give you a chance to go back and revisit your wish list and really think about how your remodeled space will work. As you develop the floor plan be sure to think about how the space will be used and what kinds of accessories and equipment you'll want to include, which can range from a big-screen TV or home theater system to a kitchen or full bathroom. A design that doesn't account for necessary cables, wiring, or plumbing could be disastrous in the end.

In general, successful remodeling projects are as much about good communication and expectations as anything else. Creating a floor plan that reflects your vision not only helps you visualize your finished basement before it is transformed, but also makes sure that your intentions are communicated and carried out.

above • The dark kitchen cabinets provide a change of pace to the otherwise light-colored walls. The tiled wall/post at the end of the kitchen contrasts with the paneled section adjacent to it.

Positioning the bar below this beam turned a liability into an asset. Covered with wood, it frames the bar area and holds recessed fixtures that light the countertop.

A Period Remodel

Strict attention to detail and the interplay between light- and dark-colored finishes combine to create something special in this period remodeled basement. The stage is set by the elegant stairs and faithfully carried throughout the entire basement. The major surfaces—walls, ceilings, and floors—are primarily honey-toned woods, dramatically set off by much darker elements.

The ceiling beams, along with the painted border, serve to divide the wide-open space into separate areas. For emphasis, the doors and openings between rooms are surrounded by dark trim. Although there are several shades of light-colored surfaces, there is, with the exception of the floor border, only one dark color. This ties everything together, preventing the space from becoming too chaotic. Although the amount of custom woodwork and trim detail certainly makes this a costly project, the concepts can be easily mimicked for much less.

right • Naturally finished wood trim and handrail cap the dark wood paneling and balusters, respectively. The stair treads seem to float on the painted risers, whereas the strongly detailed newel post anchors the handrail.

Reclaiming Wasted Space

As you plan your basement remodel be on the lookout for ways to utilize space that might otherwise go to waste. Niches and recesses in walls, under stairs, and into adjacent spaces are easy to create, but should be built during the framing stage of construction and coordinated with wiring and plumbing.

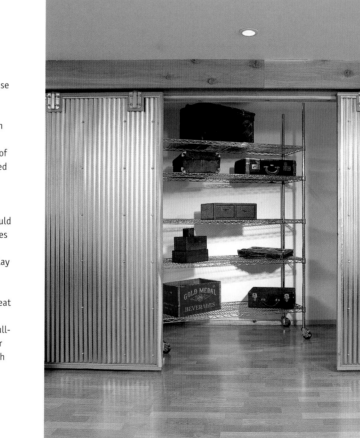

1. Hidden behind a pair of custom-built sliding doors, this triangular nook is currently used for storage. However, because the flooring is continuous, with the doors open or removed this nook can be used as part of the main space. **2.** Although it can result in angled shapes, the wide space underneath stairs allows the construction of deeper shelves. When stairs can be accessed on both sides, recesses can be built back-to-back. **3.** These recessed shelves don't intrude on the dining table, and although they are currently used for display they could put some of the most frequently used dishes within arms reach. **4.** Stair landings are a great place for recessed shelving or a display niche. To make the most of the available space, lengthen the shelves to follow the slope of the steps. **5.** Deep shelves are great for storing towels and linens, but smaller items, such as toiletries, can get lost. A pull-out drawer hung with full-extension drawer slides provides easy access to the full depth and corrals needed items.

GATHERING

A finished basement is the perfect place to create spaces where families and friends can relax, get together, and enjoy each other's company.

SPACES

Open Floor Plan versus Multiple Rooms

To determine the type of gathering space you need, think carefully about how you will use the space. Do you want a place where your immediate family can spend time together, or a place where your kids can hang out with friends? Would an outside entrance, where pets and kids can run freely in and out of the basement, make life easier? Do you entertain and crave a separate space to hold dinner parties?

Most successful basement designs begin with an open floor plan. Because basements tend to have low ceilings and limited natural light, the open plan makes spaces feel generous and airy. But an open plan doesn't mean you can't create distinct areas. Instead of full-height walls that partition off space, enlist the aid of half-walls, beams and posts, different flooring materials, and changes in ceiling height to define spaces.

One of the disadvantages of an open floor plan is noise—without walls it easily fills an open space, so try to locate quiet areas away from noisier ones. If your finished basement will include an area for quiet reading, you won't want to place it right next to the TV. And if your new space includes a kitchen and eating area for entertaining, you will want to locate it away from the kids' play space.

Of course, the entire basement space doesn't have to be wide open. To enclose private spaces, full-height walls and tight-sealing doors are totally appropriate, sometimes even necessary. For example, even though guests can stay in a pull-out sleeper in the family room, everyone is probably going to be more comfortable with a separate bedroom. A home office that is used to see clients almost certainly needs the privacy that walls provide.

top • Kids love to hang out on the floor and watch TV, so leaving open floor space makes a room kid-friendly. The soffit helps to define the end of this room, ties in with the beams, and provides a place for the cabinets to end.

above • The large beam running down the middle of this narrow room eliminates the need for a Lally column, clearing the sightlines to the end wall. Built-in cabinets and a fireplace maximize the available space, and the angled TV effectively increases the width of the room.

facing page • Bright colors, comfortable furniture, plenty of storage, and a fireplace—this basement family room is as stylish as any room on the first floor would be. Even the artwork on the mantle is color-coordinated.

A Remodeled Basement for the Entire Family

Wanting to create enough space so that the entire family would be able to use the renovated basement, a small one-story addition as well as extensive remodeling was incorporated into the plans for this basement renovation. To make room for the addition and carve out enough space for a sunken dining patio, the earth at one end of the basement was removed and a low retaining wall, along with a set of steps connecting the new patio to the yard, was constructed.

To improve traffic flow, and thereby gain additional useable space, the stairs down to the basement were reconfigured from an L-shape to a space-saving straight-run stair. This allowed the door leading outdoors to be repositioned slightly and the circulation hallway to be widened. Painting every individual room a different color draws a sharp distinction between each room, making the overall space feel larger than it really is.

facing page left • This single French door lets light penetrate the family room from the circulation hall and visa-versa. While a laminate wood floor graces the family room, a tough tile floor is appropriate for the high traffic hall.

facing page right • The one-story addition provided the opportunity for something rare in a basement space—cathedral ceilings. Although the green walls darken the room a bit, the lighter colored ceiling and floor bounce around ample light thanks to the windows and door.

left • Although narrow, these stairs are brightly lit at the top and bottom by windows. The sturdy handrail hugs close to the wall, taking up as little space as possible.

below • A pair of exterior French doors, which match their interior counterparts, provides free and easy access to the new patio. Building the patio at the same level as the basement also makes it easier to access.

Family Rooms

To overcome all the distractions that modern families face—office work, housework, homework, after-school activities, and the latest video game—the family room has to be a place where your family wants to be. A frequently used—and enjoyed—family room has something for everyone and accommodates the ways families actually interact. It's a rare moment when, all at once, the whole family gets up and says, "Let's go be together. Let's play a game." Life's usually much more spontaneous than that. The trick is to get a family "together" in the same space, with each doing his or her own thing, if necessary, and then let family interactions just happen naturally. So think about the activities that your family members enjoy and give them what they want.

Watching television still seems to be a staple of family time. Video games have only increased the time spent around the TV screen, so a well-appointed family room should acknowledge this reality. The other ubiquitous screen, the computer monitor, is also a big draw. A workstation with one or perhaps two computers is almost a must. And even though portable audio devices seem to have turned listening to music into a mostly personal affair, a "communal" stereo system still has its place in a family room.

right · Taking advantage of a particularly wide space, the fireplace and TV are placed at right angles to each other, creating two clearly separate seating groups.

facing page · Two wood-sheathed Lally columns separate the Ping-Pong table, just visible behind the wingback chair, from the seating group in this family room. The low-hanging lamps are safely located between the posts, where they aren't in danger of being bumped into.

Although board games may seem almost quaint, they still have their fans, and there's nothing quite like them to encourage family interaction. Providing an area to do art or to work on school projects might make it easier for children to turn off that TV. And don't forget reading. A nice corner to curl up with a book makes a good addition to any room.

Because various activities take place in family rooms, flooring needs may change from one place to another. Ceramic tile near the outside door shrugs off water and dirt. Carpet invites children to play on the floor. And a rich hardwood floor clearly defines the eating area.

It's important to keep in mind that one of the few things you can count on in life is that families grow up and change. A family room that fits perfectly today might be out of sync tomorrow. So think long term and plan for flexibility so your family room can respond to the inevitable.

Built-Ins

Built-ins are an increasingly popular part of remodeling projects. Although they may be more costly than stock pieces, custom built-ins offer two distinct advantages. First, of course, they can be designed to meet specific requirements and match existing features and woodwork. Built-ins also maximize the use of space. They can be constructed to span from wall to wall and reach from floor to ceiling. They also can be made to fit into small and odd-shaped spaces. This is particularly important in a basement, where nooks and crannies abound.

1. The clean lines and sharp edges of these built-in shelves are matched by the drywall corners that form the recess. The custom shelves allow the heating grills to be concealed below the bottom shelf. **2.** Combining open and closed shelving in one built-in unit makes it more flexible. Thin shelves are given a more substantial look due to the wide strip mounted on their front. This also makes the shelves stronger. **3.** The wall on either side of the door was padded out to create enough room for built-in bookshelves. Detailed to match the others in the space, two columns mark the entrance to the door and the ends of the shelves.

4. Built-in shelving doesn't have to be boring. Painting the inside of each shelf section not only creates a playful atmosphere but also provides a varied background that highlights objects of contrasting colors.

5. Designed to squeeze into a small recess, this built-in cabinet offers big storage for its size. The deep bottom drawer, which can handle larger, bulky items, has a faux two-drawer front, which keeps it in scale with the rest of the unit. Full-extension drawer slides make access easy.

FURNITURE ARRANGEMENTS

With all you might have planned for the family room, it could easily become the proverbial three-ring circus. Although you don't want your family room to feel crazed and disorganized, you do want to encourage multiple activities in the same room. With this in mind it's best to break the furniture down into several smaller groupings instead of clustering everything together. This not only separates the different activities, but allows you to choose different types of furniture and create arrangements that work best. For example, a TV is best viewed straight on, but when playing board or card games people like to circle around a table.

Another mistake to avoid, even in relatively small rooms, is to push all the furniture back against the walls. This approach puts too much distance between the furniture and makes interactions difficult. With a couch against one wall and the TV on the opposite wall, people are constantly walking back and forth in front of the TV, annoying the viewer. Pulling the furniture away from the walls into tighter arrangements and leaving room for people to pass behind and around it makes for a better functioning space and creates visual interest.

Furniture placement can even influence the size and shape of the room. To ensure that there's adequate space for the furniture you want, consider creating a room plan on a piece of graph paper. Then, using paper or cardboard cutouts, try various arrangements until you find one or more that you're satisfied with. If you have to, just "move" the walls of the room on paper.

top · This compact entertainment center puts the TV at the correct viewing height and provides plenty of storage for DVDs and videos. The paneled doors are a good match for the existing doors.

above · Some types of noise are more compatible than others. The TV can inhibit conversation and vice versa, so physically separating the television from a gaming space makes sense. The clink of glasses, the clack of pool balls, and friendly conversation are right at home with each other.

facing page · This sectional couch and matching chair make for flexible, comfortable seating, with plenty of room for people to move around. In a pinch, the lightweight chairs at the counter can be easily moved and added to the group.

Even the most carefully thought-out furniture arrangement won't work in every situation, so be flexible with your choice of furniture to make your family room flexible too. Furniture that is light-weight, or has legs with glides or casters, is easy to move around when everyone brings a friend home to play the newest video game. Tables with hidden leaves can accommodate a quiet game of solitaire or, when opened up, six wiggling children creating a Play-Doh® wonderland.

The style of the furniture is also important. A family room is supposed to be used, so stiff, formal furniture is definitely out of place. Choose a style that is conducive to all ages, and be sure to consider durable, stain-resistant fabrics. Slipcovers are a great option for a basement family room because they can be removed easily for cleaning and provide a new lease on life for an old couch.

Don't forget about furniture and accessories that can do double duty and make the space more comfortable, like ottomans, pillows, and throws. Ottomans are a great way to add extra seating in an instant or to prop up feet. Pillows and throws allow kids of all ages to cozy up on the floor with a book—or each other—for some quiet time. A desk that can house a computer for kids playing video games and for mom when it's time to pay bills offers multiple options.

When it comes to decorating, treat this space as you would any other, meaning make it feel like home. Family photos, kids' artwork, framed prints, favorite collectibles—use everything and anything to create a family room that feels familiar. As with any other room in the home, take note of who will use the space and be sure glass or treasured items are out of the reach of little fingers or bouncing balls.

top • An L-shaped sectional couch creates intimate seating that can be pulled apart and moved to make a more formal arrangement with the two pieces facing each other.

above • This barlike corner is a sports lover's dream. With a TV across the room, this counter-height table paired with high stools is perfect for watching the ball game or reading the stats in the morning paper.

facing page • Alcoves make a perfect cozy sitting area. This one is blessed with windows on three sides, adding not only views but also warmth from the sun.

A Family Room that Entertains

Before it was remodeled, this basement suffered from low ceilings, small windows, and dark wood paneling that would have made cave dwellers feel claustrophobic. But thanks to a well-thought-out design and some dramatic structural changes it was transformed into a light-filled entertainment space that welcomes friends and guests.

After lowering the floor to create sufficient headroom, the need for light was addressed. Although the basement had a southern exposure, the sun was shut out by the concrete block foundation. Using concrete saws, large holes were cut in the foundation, about 80 percent of which was removed. Engineered wood beams were installed to span the openings, which accommodated two pairs of French doors with sidelights. Light now fills the entire space.

The exterior wall wasn't the only one that was reconfigured. Much of the carrying wall that ran parallel to the stairs was removed and replaced with a flush beam hidden in the ceiling. This not only opened up the stairs at the bottom, but also set up an efficient circulation pattern, allowing the new kitchen to be accessed from both the game and seating areas.

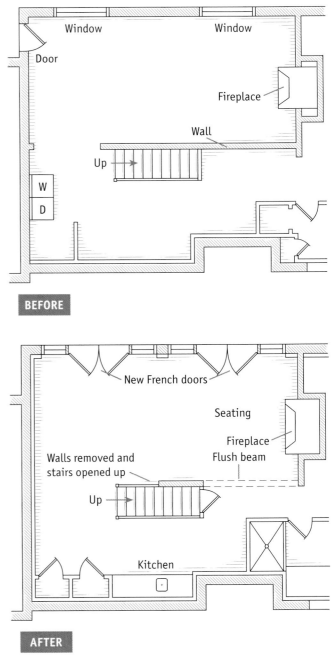

BEFORE

AFTER

left · About two-thirds of the stairs are open, allowing light from the glass door on the main level to penetrate to the back wall of the basement. The conversation grouping, located behind the solid section of the stairs, is shielded from much of the noise from the kitchenette.

left · The central stairs separate the kitchenette from the rest of the space without being too obtrusive. They also create an efficient circulation pattern because people can walk behind them. A host serving drinks or food can go to either the seating group or the pool table directly from the kitchenette. A bathroom is conveniently but discretely located at the end of the kitchen.

below · Guests arriving at the bottom of the stairs are greeted by the light and views offered by the bank of French doors. The curved railing on the stairs directs people one way or the other.

WHAT TO DO WITH THE TV

The TV is often the center of attention in a family room, so a seating group is inevitably focused around it. Depending on the size of your TV, though, it may stick out like a sore thumb and become too much of a focal point of the space.

Consider a built-in entertainment center, which can incorporate not only a TV but also shelves and cubbies for DVDs and video games. Built-ins must be considered early on in the remodeling process, though, because they are constructed in place within a wall. The dimensions of the built-in may be influenced by obstructions in the basement, from Lally columns to support beams to drainpipes or heating ducts running below the ceiling. A custom built-in might be the answer, but remember that it becomes a fixture in the room and stays in place whether you move or simply redecorate five years down the road. A stock entertainment center might suit your needs, particularly if your family likes to indulge in the latest piece of video or audio equipment.

A common way to incorporate the TV into the family room is to locate it near a fireplace, which allows these two focal points to both be enjoyed at the same time. One approach is to put the TV and fireplace side by side. However, the seating group around them may get to be so wide that it doesn't work for either one. Another strategy is to place the TV above the fireplace. Although this improves seating, it puts the TV at a less than optimal viewing angle. The best solution, if at all possible, is to create two separate seating groups.

Don't have a fireplace? It's easier than ever to add one to any room in the home by installing a prefabricated zero-clearance fireplace. Although most types mimic a conventional masonry fireplace, zero-clearance types can be installed in close proximity to combustible material (such as wood floors). Prefabs can be added during a renovation as long as there is sufficient floor space and a pathway up through the house for an adequate exhaust system. Of course, you'll need to consult your local building codes for any restrictions and plan for a fireplace early on in the remodeling process, because it needs to be positioned such that the chimney doesn't block windows on higher floors.

left · Although the TV is neatly built into a wall and there's comfortable seating, this setup would have been more successful if the main travel path from door to sofa wasn't directly in front of the viewer.

facing page · Discreetly hung on the wall, this TV takes up a minimal amount of space and allows for storage on top of the cabinet below.

The Four Layers of Lighting

Lighting professionals break lighting down into four categories: ambient, task, accent, and decorative. Each performs its own special function, and a well-lit space should use a mix of at least the first three types of lighting.

Ambient Lighting

Ambient light is a soft, general light that fills a room. It's an "indirect" type of light that is created by fixtures, called luminaries by professionals, that bounce light off of room surfaces, such as walls and ceilings. The best sources of ambient lighting are wall sconces, cove lighting, torchiere floor lamps, and indirect pendant or ceiling fixtures that shine most of their light up to the ceiling. It's good to have more than once source of ambient light to balance the lighting scheme in a room. If ambient light is the only type of light in a space, everything is likely to look "flat" and lack depth.

Task Lighting

Activities that need to be well lit and shadow free—such as reading, food preparation, and sewing—require task lighting. Best located between your head and the work surface, light sources from two directions will eliminate shadows and help minimize glare. Portable lamps work well for reading, and undercabinet lights are an excellent choice for the kitchen. Recessed and track lights can also provide task lighting, but they need to be positioned very carefully to avoid casting shadows.

Accent Lighting

Accent lighting is narrow-beam light that's focused on specific objects, such as paintings, display niches, or plants. It's usually provided by track lighting or adjustable recessed lighting. It does a poor job of general illumination but is an excellent complement to ambient lighting.

Decorative Lighting

Decorative lighting is not intended to illuminate a room, but rather to add some pizzazz or sparkle. Unlike the other types of lighting, the fixtures themselves are often more important than the light they produce.

Wine-Tasting Spaces

The dark spaces and cool, even temperatures found in basements make them a good place to store wine. If you're a connoisseur, of course, you may want to construct a separate, climate-controlled room. If you want to take advantage of special purchases and just need to store a modest number of bottles over a shorter period, an alcove or small room against a cooler outside wall may do just fine. Either way, you may want to include a private place to enjoy your wine near where it's stored. You can create a unique atmosphere that enhances the experience.

1. Separated from the work area of the kitchenette, wine bottles can be retrieved from this built-in storage wall without disrupting the food preparation.
2. This whimsical wine-tasting alcove, complete with wine steward, also has a practical side, with its mix of storage options, serving counter, and overhead glass rack.

3. Custom storage drawers outfitted with full-extension slides let you view what's in stock without lifting up a single bottle.
4. The controlled environment ensures that wine in this well-stocked basement wine cellar is kept at precisely the right temperature. Wine can be store individually or by the case on the rustic shelving.
5. One wall of wine and the other a vineyard make this space a wine-lover's paradise. The wrought iron chandelier and ornate table and chairs add to the old-world charm.

ADDING A KITCHENETTE AND BATH

Because a successful family room should cater to everyone's needs, think about adding a kitchen and/or bathroom. Neither of these needs to be fully appointed places for creating a gourmet meal or lounging in a spa-like atmosphere, but including at least a food and drink center and a half-bath will keep family members happy and eliminate countless trips up and down the stairs.

If you decide that one or both of these options is important, again take cues from how your family lives. If you go the food-prep route, what do you want your "kitchen" to provide: simply a place for getting snacks and beverages or a place to actually do some cooking, serving, and cleaning up? Do you need a place to sit down and eat? Today's smaller appliances make incorporating a small-scale cooking and eating center easier than ever. Consider building in a counter area that includes an undercounter refrigerator, wine cooler, and bar sink. Don't forget about a place to store dishware—paper, plastic, or glass—as well as trash and recycling receptacles. Bar stools that can be pulled up to the counter are great for keeping the kitchen and eating area confined to one smaller area.

As for bathroom facilities, a family room bathroom doesn't have to be large; in fact, a half-bath will do quite nicely and can usually be tucked away in a corner of the family room. If at all possible, try to locate the bathroom in such a way that it doesn't open directly into the family room. If that can't be done, hang the door so that it screens the water closet when it's open.

above • The 42-in.-high section of counter screens the potentially messy sink from the rest of the family room, whereas the goose-neck faucet eases cleanup. Throw rugs cushion the hard but durable tile floor.

left • A family room bathroom doesn't require lots of storage for toiletries, so a pedestal sink, which takes up less space than a vanity counter and sink, is a nice choice. The freestanding cabinet provides plenty of storage for towels and cleaning supplies.

left · This basement kitchen has everything it needs—full-size refrigerator, range, microwave, sink, ample cabinetry—to serve a full meal. The soffit that runs around the perimeter of the space conceals both the heating ducts and the recessed lighting.

below · With private access, plenty of light, and a clear definition of interior spaces, this in-law suite (a bedroom is tucked off to one side) is as comfortable as if it were on a main living floor.

Kitchens

When planning a kitchen for your basement, space may be at a premium, so choose an efficient or compact layout and think carefully about the number of appliances and amount of counter and cabinet space you really need. Although you may need to install a small kitchen, you don't have to compromise on quality: Buy well-made, durable products and materials.

1. Although this single-wall drink center is open to the rest of the space, the white cabinetry that's flush with a side wall allows it to blend in with the background, minimizing its visual impact. 2. Good ventilation is important in basement kitchens and the powerful vent hood above this commercial-style range ensures that cooking odors and fumes won't get trapped in the space. Flush plywood cabinet doors provide a modern look that blends well with the sleek stainless steel surfaces of the range. 3. Low-backed and delicately proportioned, the silver metal and light-colored wood of these stools echo the bar and counter supports. They only have footrests at the front, as they are mainly intended to be used while seated at the counter. 4. When dealing with tight spaces, consider fixtures that are custom-made to accommodate the space. This counter and integrated double-bowl sink are less than the standard 2-ft. depth, allowing them to squeeze into a corner. 5. An appliance garage helps keep infrequently used pieces of equipment out of the way. The under-cabinet light that's thoughtfully placed in front of this one will light up its dark interior. 6. To maximize storage space, the wall cabinets in this efficient, single-wall kitchen go all the way to the ceiling, as does the refrigerator.

Entertaining Areas

Basement remodeling projects often seem to revolve around children and family. But what if the children are grown and gone? Or what if you just don't have any children? There is no rule that says that adults can't have the run of the basement, and if you're looking for a place to entertain your widening circle of friends, the basement might just fit the bill.

Why, you say, do you need to relegate adult entertaining to the basement? You don't, of course. But one of the biggest reasons to consider it is so you don't have to compromise the way you live day to day for an occasional party. And a dedicated "party" space could also be reserved for small groups, again away from the dishes in the sink or extra magazines spread out on the coffee table in the main-floor family room. Remodeling your basement will let you have your cake and eat it too.

A relatively wide-open basement allows you to custom-design the space to accommodate the specific needs that come with entertaining, most important among them creating good flow and encouraging interaction. Narrow doorways and halls create bottlenecks, so eliminate them whenever possible or make them at least 4 ft. wide. Also, make sure that there is plenty of space around the furniture so that two people can easily pass each other.

To maintain visual openness, full-height walls, of course, are to be avoided at all costs. However, for maximum flexibility, use half-walls sparingly and separate areas with furniture. Most conversation takes place in small groups, so plan several intimate seating arrangements, perhaps centered around and pulled tight to coffee tables. Chairs that are easy to move allow guests to rearrange the groupings to suit the flow of conversation.

top • The sleek, black counter and upholstered stools set the tone for a decidedly adult-friendly space. The wide-open floor plan ensures that friends and partygoers can mingle easily.

right • While floor pillows aren't for everyone, they can provide flexible—and fast—seating when a board game, or perhaps a tray of hors d'oeuvres, is put on the coffee table.

above • With a push of a button the reason for orienting the seating group diagonally becomes apparent as the screen descends and the topic of conversation turns to the movie.

left • This comfortable seating group is interestingly organized along a diagonal axis created by the built-in and carried through by the coffee and end tables. The ceiling helps define the seating area and prevents it from feeling like it's just floating in space.

Game Tables

Playing games on a folding card table with rickety legs and a warped top that's occasionally dragged out of the closet is just no fun. Instead, make a game table a permanent, attractive addition to your room. When shopping for a game table, keep your room's décor in mind and, of course, the type of games you will play and the number of players who need to be accommodated. You might like a table that has an integral game board and storage for game pieces and accessories. To make sure a particular table is comfortable, try it out. Sit down and pull a chair up to it.

1. The backgammon board is an inlaid design feature on the top of this game table. Flip the top over to find a chessboard. The relatively low height of this table makes it difficult to pull the chairs right up to and under the table. 2. Most table leaves fold down, but not so in this clever design. When closed, this table masquerades as a handsome end table. Lifting up the top reveals its true nature—a card table replete with green felt surface.

3. A dinner table one minute—remove the top and it's a fully appointed gaming table the next. This octagonal table offers seating for eight. The sturdy pedestal base keeps it stable during the height of activity. 4. The pedestal base of this octagonal table keeps the legs tucked up under the top. The top has four shorter and four longer sides, which creates ample room for a friendly game of bridge. 5. Built for an intimate game for two, this elegant game table could easily double as a bistro table where refreshments are served after the game is over.

COOKING AND SERVING

If you're entertaining a small group—four to six, for example—preparing and serving the meal will be similar to the everyday routine. However, as the numbers increase, the menu typically gets simpler, or perhaps the food is even catered.

Obviously you aren't going to host the same kind of party with the same number of people every time. But you do need to think about what you're most likely to do and subsequently what your appliance and space needs will be, including commercial-style stove, double oven, full-size refrigerator, sink, dishwasher, and multiple serving counters.

above • With an undercounter refrigerator and bar sink, this station offers an additional place to have drinks available. The lack of overhead cabinets is a plus in this case, as it lessens the overall impact on the space.

right • Modern color-matching techniques were used to mix a paint that is the exact color as the seats of these bar stools. As a result, the stools become an integral part of this handsome color scheme.

facing page • Rich detailing and a subdued color palette in tones of cinnamon and black create a classic backdrop for a game of pool. The built-up crown molding at the ceiling helps to visually expand this relatively small space.

When laying out this space, think of it as you would your main-floor kitchen—that is, make it function efficiently and keep most-used gadgets within easy reach. And don't forget that people tend to congregate in a kitchen no matter where it is, so be sure there is enough counter space for leaning and flow around the kitchen area for the guests and hosts doing the prep work, cooking, and cleaning up. The goal with any gathering is for the host to feel like part of the party and enjoy the guests, so consider a long counter that faces the room that can handle a number of trays, provide space for refilling bowls, and help keep the hosts engaged. Consider, too, a separate bar area with a small sink for mixing drinks and rinsing glasses.

Unless you will be hosting primarily formal, sit-down dinners, when designing a space for entertaining you have to account for the accompanying quirks of serving and eating food and drinks. Planning for multiple counter surfaces—near the prep area, on a bar, or around a drink station—will help to alleviate traffic jams. Portable counter surfaces, such as nesting or occasional tables, ottomans, and eating tables, can be called into service, providing additional space when a party is in full swing.

Bar Stools

Bar stools come in a wide array of styles and shapes, but the overriding consideration should be practical: how they will be used. If you want people to linger on the stools, you might want to opt for cushioned seats as opposed to wood or metal types. A back can also make the seat feel secure and allow sitters to lounge a bit. Swivel seats allow people to easily turn toward each other and other areas of the room. Of course, height is an option that needs to be considered as well. Once you address these needs, turn to the myriad design options to pick the style that works with the rest of your décor.

1. These round, padded stools are covered with the same leather that's installed on the front of the bar. It's an unusual detail that absorbs sound and protects the knees of the people sitting at the bar. 2. The wooden frames and straightforward design of these bar stools blend well with the casual style of this kitchenette. Two sets of stretchers offer foot-rest options for kids and adults alike. 3. These stylish wooden stools are as much art as practical furniture. Their shape is perfect in the geometrically outfitted kitchen. 4. Neat, clean lines make these stools an excellent choice for this no-nonsense bar. Their wide bases create stability, and even though they don't swivel, the leather seats and footrests make it easy for people to turn to either side. 5. The high backs of these upholstered bar stools provide excellent support and allow people to lean back without fear of sliding off. The stainless steel footrests, unlike wood, won't show scuff marks or scratches.

Home Theaters

With the advent of more affordable wide-screen and high-definition TVs, DVDs, and surround-sound speaker options, home theaters are being incorporated into even the most modest of finished basements. But what exactly is a home theater? When does a TV room or that seating group around the family room TV morph into a full-fledged home theater? Can a home theater be created within a family room or does it require a separate room? Actually there's no one right answer. Although a dedicated room certainly makes it easier to create a home theater atmosphere, a perfectly fine home theater experience can be created within a larger space. A successful home theater depends more on careful space planning and layout than anything else.

above • Entertaining friends sometimes means relaxing conversation around the fireplace one minute and watching a special movie the next. Swivel chairs make it easy to change venues.

right • When the focus should be on your guests and not the television, a floor-to-ceiling curtain completely hides this large-screen TV.

SHAPE THE SPACE

The first question that's often asked when thinking about a home theater is, "How big a screen should I have?" The response is often another question: "How big is the space?" Because the size of the room—or, more precisely, the distance you sit away from the screen—affects the size of the screen, determining the viewing distance is a good place to start.

One of the things that creates an enjoyable home theater experience is the visual impact of the image on the screen. Like in a movie theater, you want to be drawn into what you're watching and forget about your surroundings. However, if you sit too far away from the screen much of that impact will be lost. You might as well be watching just another big TV. On the other hand, sitting too close is also a problem, because you'll be able to see the structure of the image—the lines or pixels that make up the picture.

TV Viewing Distances

The viewing distances shown here provide a suggested range for viewing wide-screen analog and high-definition TVs. Ideal viewing distances vary due to differences in signal quality, the surroundings, and personal preferences.

Wide-Screen Analog TVs

Screen Size (in width)	Minimum Distance	Maximum Distance
30 in.	7 ft. 6 in.	12 ft. 6 in.
36 in.	9 ft. 0 in.	15 ft. 0 in.
40 in.	10 ft. 0 in.	16 ft. 6 in.
48 in.	12 ft. 0 in.	20 ft. 0 in.
56 in.	14 ft. 0 in.	23 ft. 0 in.

Wide-Screen HDTVs

Screen Size (in width)	Minimum Distance	Maximum Distance
30 in.	5 ft. 0 in.	10 ft. 0 in.
36 in.	6 ft. 0 in.	12 ft. 0 in.
40 in.	6 ft. 6 in.	13 ft. 6 in.
48 in.	8 ft. 0 in.	16 ft. 0 in.
56 in.	9 ft. 6 in.	18 ft. 6 in.

Taking into account field of view, as well as visual clarity, proper viewing distances are calculated using the width, not the diagonal length, of the screen. As a rule of thumb, for standard (analog) wide-screen TVs the nearest viewing distance should be about three times the width of the screen and the farthest distance about five times the width. So, the appropriate viewing distances for a screen that is 40 in. wide is between about 10 ft. and 16 ft. 6 in.

The figures change somewhat for high-definition televisions. The finer detail available with high definition supports closer viewing. The minimum distance shrinks to two times the width and the maximum to four times the width, so a 40-in. screen can be comfortably viewed from 6 ft. 6 in. to 13 ft. 6 in. away.

With the viewing distances established, you can determine how deep a room or space needs to be for a specific screen size. Continuing with the high-definition example, a 14-ft.-deep room is adequate. However, in practice it's best to add a few feet to allow people to pass behind, not in front of, the viewers when moving about the room. More important, if you are planning to add surround sound you'll need the extra space for the speakers that are placed behind the last seat. A room or space about 18 ft. deep would be a good choice in this case.

Next you need to determine the width of the room. Acoustics enters into the picture here. Many factors influence the way sound reacts in a room, but prime among them is room shape. As a general rule, a home theater room should be rectangular. Most important, avoid a square room, because this shape is very conducive to creating sound-distorting echoes. For the same reason, try to avoid spaces where the length is twice the width. A ratio of about one to one and a half is optimal. If you're incorporating a home theater into an open space, bookcases, movable panels or screens, or heavy curtains can be used to create the required shape.

Ceiling height also affects acoustics. For the best performance, ceiling height should be about 1.4 times the width or 1.9 times the length of the room. A room with an 8-ft. ceiling should be about 12 ft. wide. Obviously, the height of basement ceilings is difficult to change, so to address acoustical shortcomings a home theater may be the perfect place for that hung ceiling with acoustical tiles. Breaking up the ceiling with a soffit or changing ceiling height may also improve sound quality.

right • The fireplace, beamed ceiling, and comfortable seating make this room feel more like a family room than a home theater. The atmosphere completely changes, however, when the overhead lights are turned off and the heavy, dark curtain is opened.

facing page • A built-in platform creates two-tiered seating and gives this space the experience of a movie theater. This approach is not possible without ceilings that are at least 8 ft. high.

Entertainment Centers

Simplify the task of choosing an entertainment center by first determining whether a freestanding or a built-in unit is right for you. As a general rule, custom built-in cabinetry is more expensive than stock pieces, but that's not always the case. It is always true, however, that it's much more difficult, if not impossible, to take a built-in unit with you when you move. Another important issue is flexibility. Because the size, shape, and thickness of TVs are constantly changing, it's important that an entertainment center, whether it's custom-made or a stock unit, be designed with the future in mind and constructed so that it can be altered as needed.

1. Out of sight, out of mind—at least that's the idea. Many entertainment centers have sliding, tambour, or pocket doors that, when closed, make the TV disappear. 2. Flat-panel TVs are very thin and fit easily in standard-depth shelves or cabinets. This TV seems to float in the middle of the open shelving, but a little investigation reveals the trick. A commercially available mount secures the TV to the wall and also allows the TV to be pulled away from the wall and swiveled left or right for easy viewing.

3. This finely detailed stock unit, with tight-fitting drawers and doors and stainless steel pulls, has the look of a custom piece. The mix of closed storage below and open shelves above completes this well-thought-out design. 4. A custom-built entertainment center like this one can take advantage of odd-shaped spaces. The components are hidden behind a door to the right of the TV, and four shallow drawers at the bottom of the unit provide easy-access storage. Of course, the tight-fitting, fixed frame around the TV makes it impossible to house larger TVs.

SOUNDLY FURNISHED

In addition to your personal taste, sound is going to influence the furnishings you choose for your home theater. When sound waves bounce around a room they cause distortion. Using soft furnishings will absorb sound and eliminate as many hard, sound-reflecting surfaces as possible.

When it comes to the floor, ceramic and resilient tiles are out. Wood and laminate flooring are also not good choices. Wall-to-wall carpet is the ideal flooring material. However, if the space already has a wood or tile floor, or if you just don't like carpet, areas rugs can be used.

There are a number of ways to reduce the sound-reflecting characteristics of walls. Hanging tapestries or quilts are excellent sound absorbers. Paintings are helpful, but only if they're not framed behind glass. Shelves filled with books and heavy drapes over windows and doors are other options.

The right kind of furniture is also important. Choose chairs and sofas with soft upholstery and avoid furniture that has a lot hard surfaces, such as glass-topped coffee tables and furniture with metal legs.

Because it's not uncommon to spend two hours or longer watching a movie in a home theater, choose furniture that provides adequate support, without being too hard. On the other hand, an "overstuffed" couch that's too soft may be uncomfortable and hard to get up and out of. To accommodate personal preferences, consider more than one type or style of seating in your home theater: a couch or love seat, an easy chair, and a straight-backed chair, for example. Also, don't forget about end and coffee tables, where drinks and snacks can be in easy reach.

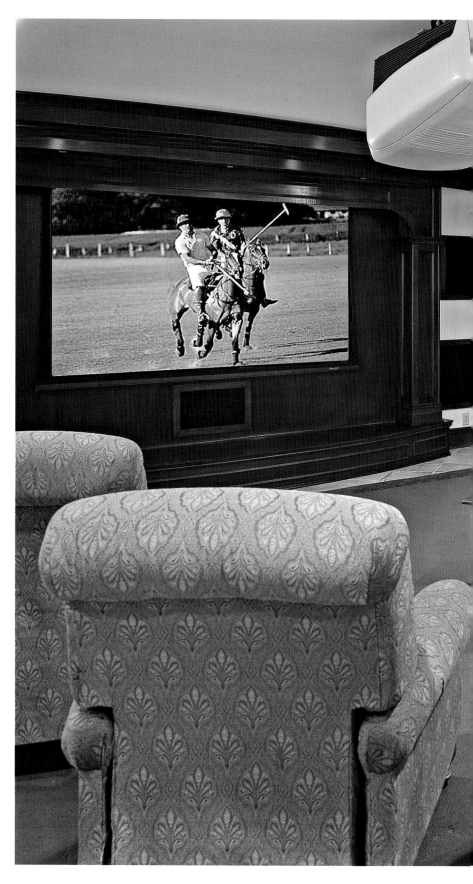

above · Multiple smaller TVs mounted in different locations on the walls ensure that everyone seated has a good viewing angle.

Planning for Speaker Wiring

To create an authentic surround-sound home theater experience you will need at least five speakers. Three speakers are positioned in the front of the room—one each in the center, right, and left of the room. Two speakers are placed to the right and left behind the viewer. The one subwoofer has no fixed position and its best location can be determined by trial and error. All those speakers mean a lot of wiring. A little planning will make sure you use the right type of speaker wiring and that it's conveniently located.

• Buy the best-quality shielded cable you can afford to minimize interference.

• Avoid bundling wires together, coiling them, or placing them near power cords, which increases interference and diminishes signal quality.

• Keep wires as short as possible; test the equipment before trimming them down to final length.

• Try to plan the speaker placement before the room is finished and run wire to the proper locations through the walls during framing. Be sure to use wire that is rated for in-wall use.

• To avoid the exposed cables that are required with freestanding speakers, consider installing in-wall or in-ceiling mounted speakers.

• Hide wires behind baseboards or ceiling trim that's built out away from the wall to create a channel.

• Conceal "flat" speaker cable, which is as thin as a credit card and can turn sharp corners, under carpet. It's even fairly inconspicuous attached directly to the wall near the baseboard, and can run up and over doors along the casing.

Some people like to watch movies close to the screen, whereas others prefer to be farther away. You can accommodate different preferences by placing seating at varying distances from the screen.

Incandescent versus Fluorescent Lighting

One of the first decisions you'll have to make when buying fixtures is the type of bulb to choose. Bulbs, called lamps in the industry, come in two general types: incandescent and fluorescent. The light that is produced by lamps is rated by the Color Rendering Index for how accurately it renders colors. A higher number on the scale, which goes from 1 to 100, indicates better color accuracy. Light is rated on the Kelvin temperature scale for how "warm" or "cool" it appears. Warmer colors, such as reds and yellows, have lower color temperatures, and cooler, bluish tones have higher readings.

STANDARD INCANDESCENT
$

- Inexpensive and readily available
- Produced in a wide range of wattages
- Easily dimmed
- Relatively short life—about 750 hours
- Light yellows when dimmed
- The least energy-efficient lamp available
- Ballast in inexpensive lamps may hum or buzz

COMPACT FLUORESCENT
$$

- Long life—about 10,000 to 20,000 hours
- Energy efficient—gives three to five times the light output per watt compared to standard incandescent
- Produces less heat than incandescent
- Doesn't change color when dimmed
- Improved color rendition and reduced size
- Newer types have built-in ballast
- Light output diminishes with age
- Larger than standard incandescents and may not fit in all fixtures
- Light quality is usually slightly different than incandescent light

HALOGEN (OR QUARTZ)
$$

- Longer life than incandescents—about 2,500 to 3,000 hours
- More energy efficient than standard incandescent
- Smaller fixtures than most other types
- Light can be focused to a narrow beam
- Light yellows and life can be shortened when dimmed
- Can get very hot—fires have been attributed to some types
- Hot bulbs should not be touched without gloves

LOW VOLTAGE
$$$

- Long life—about 10,000 hours
- Uses 12v current and reduces potential for shocks
- Produces about two and a half times more light than a 110v fixture
- Fixtures are expensive—about two to four times as much as conventional fixtures
- Most need a separate transformer to reduce the 110v line current down to 12v

This home theatre has it all—multiple light sources, finely detail woodwork, built-in speakers, and fabric-covered walls with matching curtain. The arrangement of the plush seats is comfortable for both watching movies and dishing about them afterward.

LIGHTS PLEASE

When it comes to lighting a home theater, a basement disadvantage—being light-challenged—turns into a plus. Natural light, or rather too much of it, is not desirable in a home theater. It can cause bothersome glare and reflections, so a lot of effort often goes into eliminating it. If you choose a windowless corner of your basement to house your home theater you've effectively done away with that issue. And small basement windows are easy to deal with. Heavy curtains, blinds, or even interior shutters block out most, if not all, daylight. Of course, home theaters can't be totally left in the dark. With daylight effectively out of the picture, artificial lighting is a must. Proper lighting will enhance the screen image and create the right atmosphere.

Most types of televisions, with the exception of front-projection TVs, do okay with normal room lighting. But a successful home theater re-creates the feeling of walking into a movie theater, complete with soft overhead lighting and wall sconces. As showtime approaches the overhead lights go dim and then out. When the movie begins the wall sconces are dimmed, but not turned all the way off.

To capture this movie-theater feeling you can use the light layering technique mentioned on p. 12. First, avoid harsh direct overhead lights. Choose indirect ceiling fixtures spaced so that they light the ceiling evenly, or cove lighting along the tops of the walls. For the walls, pick sconces with dark shades and open bottoms that direct the light up and down in widening cones. Softly light the wall behind the screen. For an added touch direct a few accent spots on wall-hung paintings or artwork, or mimic the floor lighting used in theaters with decorative string lights installed along the baseboard. Of course, all the lighting fixtures should be controlled with dimmers, not on/off switches. Watching TV in the dark can cause eyestrain.

Although proper lighting techniques can reduce glare and reflections, there are a couple of additional measures that help. The same soft, nonreflecting surfaces that absorb sound waves also absorb light waves. In addition, walls should be dark or neutral colors. Use paint with a flat finish or nonshiny wall paper. This not only improves the light quality, but also enhances the theater-like atmosphere.

left · The projection screen in this home theater drops down from a soffit in the ceiling. The electronic equipment and DVDs, as well as a wide-screen TV, are built into the wall behind the screen.

facing page · A perfect setting for movie watching is established by the dim light of this home theater. The mood is enhanced by the candles, although caution should always be the watchword with any open flame inside a room.

Lighting a Home Theater

There's no doubt about it, this room was designed expressly as a home theater. The owners went to great lengths to re-create the plush environment of early theaters while paying attention to the technical aspects of good home theater design. The muted colors of the fabric-covered walls and wall-to-wall carpet set the right mood for movie watching and, along with the rectangular shape of the room, help create good acoustics. The highly finished posts and false ceiling beams evoke a bygone era and serve to visually break up the long room.

Special attention was paid to lighting the space. The wall sconces installed on the posts add to the theaterlike atmosphere. Those near the screen, which is appropriately set against a dark background, softly light the screen when the lights are turned down. Cove lights run around the entire perimeter of the room and are the perfect way to create indirect, ambient lighting. Additional ambient lighting is supplied by the same cove lights hidden in the recessed portion of the ceiling, completing a balanced, well-thought-out lighting scheme.

right · This home theater is appropriately lit with indirect ambient lighting. Taking advantage of the highly detailed trim, cove lighting is hidden behind the crown molding at the intersection of the walls and ceilings as well as in the ceiling recess in the center of the room. Wall sconces allow for more light when it's needed.

below · The only place this home theater strays from good design is with the metal and glass-topped tables. However, given their placement behind the sound-absorbent couches, their negative effects on the sound quality are probably minimal.

ACTIVITY

Spaces dedicated to one activity are hard to come by in any home,

but a basement can change this. It may just be the perfect spot for that

home gym, kid's playroom, craft space, or laundry room.

SPACES

Home Fitness Rooms

Home is where the heart is. And more and more frequently these days, home is also where the heart gets a good workout. For many a trip to the local health club is just one more stop in an already jam-packed schedule. Why not just walk down a flight of stairs to your very own gym, open 24 hours a day, 7 days a week?

Although a home gym might sound like a dream come true, take a few minutes to think about whether one is right for you before you run out and buy all the latest equipment. Once you make that decision, there are a few things to consider before you actually start to design the space. First, determine what it is you're trying to accomplish. Do you want to lose weight or tone up? Although most exercise programs incorporate both, you may want to emphasize one or the other, and your decision will affect the type of equipment you buy, which in turn will help determine how you configure the space.

Your personal preferences are another important consideration that will influence the choice of exercise equipment. What types of exercise do you like to do? If you hate the thought of climbing steps or find it incredibly boring, a stair-stepping machine is probably not for you. Perhaps you don't feel comfortable riding a bicycle on busy streets.

A stationary bike provides low-impact exercise in the comfort of your home. You may want to outfit a home fitness room to complement the type of exercise you already do. If you're a walker, a ski machine adds a little variety.

left • With the bigger equipment placed at the ends, the smaller bench near the center, and the exercise balls and dumbbells neatly stored against the walls, the middle of the room is open, making it easy to move from station to station. The full-wall mirror visually doubles the space.

facing page • The typical exercise equipment layout is regular and regimented, but thanks to a large room this fitness space has good flow. Individual workout stations are connected by a sinuous band of wood flooring, and a comfortable seating area offers a place to rest afterward.

SPACE REQUIREMENTS

Think first about what pieces of equipment you want (both now and in the future, because your exercise routine will likely change), and compare the space requirements of each piece. Some are long and narrow, others more compact, and still others may need to be accessed on two or more sides. Keep in mind that many pieces need additional space while they're being used.

When it comes to home fitness spaces, basements do offer a number of advantages, particularly if you're going to devote the entire room or a large portion of it to exercise. In a narrow room an efficient approach is to line the equipment along one wall, placing the longer equipment near the ends. This opens up the middle of the room and, with easy access to wall plugs, keeps electrical cords out of the way. An open floor plan means you have the ability to create stations and to keep the floor clear for stretching or yoga. Wider rooms may permit equipment to be placed on two or more walls.

In some instances, though, the physical limitations of the space may impact equipment choices, particularly ceiling height. Most equipment is designed to be used in spaces with a standard 8-ft. ceiling. If your basement ceiling is only around 7 ft., some pieces might not fit. Another factor to consider is functional height. For example, many treadmill platforms are about 6 in. off the floor. When someone who is 6 ft. 2 in. stands on the platform, his or her head is only 4 in. from a 7-ft. ceiling; add to that any bouncing when running and that person's head could actually hit the ceiling. Even if the ceiling isn't quite that low, the psychological impact of a less than full-height ceiling can make using certain equipment uncomfortable.

top • A large mirror combined with the sharply contrasting blue wall makes it appear as if this narrow fitness room has a separate alcove. The mirror reveals that the equipment is efficiently arranged in a single line.

right • The storage alcove and built-in shelving keep smaller exercise equipment and accessories neatly tucked away but easy to get at. Furnishings with moisture-resistant fabrics, such as this built-in leather couch, make it easy to keep the furniture clean and dry.

Home Exercise Equipment

There is a wide range of exercise equipment designed for home fitness. If you haven't used a piece of equipment that you're considering purchasing, take out a two-week membership at your local gym so you can try the different types and make a more informed buying decision.

Aerobic Fitness Equipment

• Stationary bicycles work the legs through the pedaling motion of a bicycle. Some models are used sitting upright, others recumbent (reclined).

• Treadmills let you walk or run at varying speeds. Some models simulate inclines of various degrees, and many incorporate timers.

• Ski machines simulate the motion of cross-country (also called Nordic) skiing and exercise the legs and arms simultaneously.

• Stairsteppers/climbers duplicate the motion of climbing up a flight of stairs. Some add upper-body exercise by simulating a pull-up climbing motion with the arms.

• Elliptical trainers are sort of a cross between a ski machine and a stairstepper, and put your legs and feet through a circular, up-and-down motion.

• Rowing machines work the back, arms, and legs.

• Aerobic riders exercise the arms and legs simultaneously through a push/pull motion.

Strength-Training Equipment

• Free weights, sometimes called "barbells" and "dumbbells," are among the most common forms of home exercise equipment.

• Multistation machines, also known as "home gyms," typically use resistance created by either rubber bands or cables attached to plated weights or flexible poles.

• Bands and tubing are lightweight ways to strength train at your home or office or while on the road.

Miscellaneous Fitness Equipment

• Heart-rate monitors provide motivation and feedback and help you monitor exercise intensity.

• Exercise or stability balls have proven very effective for balance and flexibility training.

• Pilates equipment is based on the patents of exercise pioneer Joseph Pilates and targets both strength and flexibility benefits.

A Lally column or two can cause problems in an exercise space. The best way to deal with these is to work them into the equipment layout. For example, if your basement has two or more columns in a row, align the equipment with them, in a single line. By alternating longer pieces with shorter ones you probably can fit two pieces between each pair of Lallys.

Because you'll be spending some portion of your time exercising on the floor, you want to make sure the floor finish is durable, easy to clean, and soft underfoot. Resilient flooring—such as vinyl, linoleum, cork, and rubber—are the best choices. Spills and dripping perspiration can be wiped up easily, and these flooring types provide a measure of cushioning and help reduce noise. Although carpet is soft and absorbs sound, it also absorbs water, is hard to clean, and may over time make your exercise room smell like a gym. Also, the fibers may get into some types of equipment. Carpet is appropriate in some places, such as the stretching area. Ceramic tile is easy to clean but is hard underfoot and noisy. If the space already has tile, use area rugs and mats on top of it to provide some relief.

Tips for Buying Exercise Equipment

Shopping for home exercise equipment can be a daunting task. Here are some tips to help you evaluate and choose the equipment that's best for you and your exercise program.

• **Set a budget.** Determine how much money you want to spend and then spread it among different pieces of equipment. A good strategy is to allocate a large portion of your budget to a high-quality piece of aerobic equipment—a treadmill or elliptical trainer, for example—and buy less-expensive strength equipment. But always buy the best quality you can afford.

• **Try before you buy.** The only way for you to evaluate how a particular piece of equipment feels to you is to try it out. When you go shopping wear appropriate shoes and clothing. Does the piece operate smoothly and feel solid as you work on it? Can you adjust it to a position that's comfortable and feels natural?

• **Ask questions.** Don't be embarrassed to ask questions, particularly if you're unsure about how to adjust or properly use a piece of equipment. You're likely to get better advice and service from a store that specializes in exercise equipment than from a department store. Also ask about warranties, return policies, and repair service. Some retailers will allow you to try a piece of equipment for a specified period of time.

• **Check out the accessories.** Some equipment comes complete with accessories, such as heart-rate monitors, calories-burned displays, timers, and televised displays, all at a price. If you don't think you're really going to use such bells and whistles, you'll get better value for your money by purchasing a more basic machine.

• **Consider used equipment.** You can make your budget go farther or buy higher-quality equipment than you might otherwise be able to afford by buying used equipment. The Internet makes this approach particularly easy, but shop carefully and look for equipment that is in excellent condition and working order. Keep in mind that manufacturers' warranties will probably not come with used equipment.

above · Like many basement rooms, this one does double duty. Although it's relatively small, it still manages to combine space for exercise and relaxation.

left · Separate but together aptly describes this remodeled basement split between playroom and exercise space. Kids and parents keep an eye on each other through the large window while enjoying their own activities.

facing page · This multistation workout machine makes the most of a very small space. To provide enough ceiling clearance for this tall piece of equipment, the ducts are routed to the perimeter of the space.

CREATE AN UPBEAT ATMOSPHERE

To help keep your exercise regimen from becoming boring and drudgery, include features that make the time pass pleasantly.

Start with light. Employ light-layering techniques to create a very bright but diffusely lit space. Close-fit ceiling fixtures and cove lighting are good options. Concentrate additional light with recessed down-lights near the exercise equipment so digital readouts are easy to see. Keep the layout of the equipment in mind as you plan the location and type of lighting fixtures. If, for example, you're working with free weights lying on a bench or stretching on the floor, it can be distracting to have a light shining directly in your eyes. Wall sconces are more appropriate in these locations. Of course, all the lights should be controlled with dimmers.

Mirrors are a fundamental part of a fitness space and offer several benefits. Their reflective surfaces bounce light around the room and they visually expand a space. And, of course, mirrors are for looking into. By placing a mirror in front of the free weight station you can make sure you're using proper form.

right · Exercising at home can be a family affair. Here mom or dad can work out and keep an eye on the kids at the same time. Children love to imitate their parents, so not only do mom and dad get a chance to stay fit, but they can set a good example as well.

facing page · Light-colored floors and ceilings and full-wall mirrors in the equipment alcove work to make this exercise space feel bright and spacious. Putting the machines into the alcove leaves a lot of open space for floor work.

When incorporating a home gym into a basement, be sure you've dealt with the moisture often found in basements. Vigorous exercise pumps a lot of moisture into the air and air conditioning and/or dehumidification systems need to be the proper size to handle this additional load. Even with proper ventilation there may be times when you'd like some concentrated relief. A simple fan may be just what you need. Get a model on a rolling stand that can be adjusted to different heights.

Two other creature comforts—music and television—should be planned into a fitness space. Provide a central but out of the way place for the audio equipment, but position the television so it can be seen from multiple workstations by placing it on a movable or swivel stand. Make sure all audio equipment and TVs are located so that their remote controls work from the various exercise stations.

Flooring

When choosing flooring, consider how a particular space will be used. Some types of flooring are hard underfoot and unforgiving, whereas others are soft or resilient. Some reflect sound and light, whereas some absorb them. And, of course, the flooring you end up installing must work with the room's décor.

VINYL

VINYL
$

- Easy to install
- Resilient but thin; depending on how it's installed, can be supple underfoot
- Available in both tile and sheet forms and in a wide array of colors and patterns
- High-quality vinyl is durable and easy to clean; low-end vinyl can fade or yellow
- Joints in vinyl tiles allow water to penetrate; sheet goods have fewer seams

LINOLEUM
$$

- A natural material made from a mix of linseed oil, rosin, wood, and cork powder
- Available in a wide range of colors and patterns
- Very durable; doesn't show scuffs or scratches

- Resilient but thin; depending on how it's installed, can be supple underfoot
- Naturally biodegradable

CORK
$$$

- A natural material that's sustainably produced
- Very comfortable underfoot
- Available in tile and plank forms
- Colors are available from some manufacturers
- Prone to denting, cutting, and fading
- Can be refinished

WOOD
$$

- Sealing and staining accentuates the natural beauty of wood grain
- Comfortable underfoot
- Solid wood shrinks and swells with changes in humidity level; excessive water can buckle wood
- Can be refinished

BAMBOO

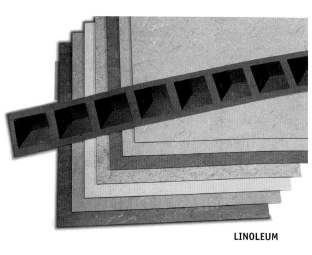

LINOLEUM

CERAMIC TILE

- Engineered wood flooring—made with a center core of hardwood, plywood, or HDF (high-density fiberboard) and a finish veneer—is more stable than solid wood but can only be refinished a limited number of times

LAMINATE
$-$$

- Manufactured material similar to countertop laminates
- Available in a wide range of colors and patterns
- High-quality laminates are very durable and some are resistant to water
- Cannot be refinished
- Available in planks, strips, and tiles; can be glued down or snapped together to make a "floating" floor

BAMBOO
$$$

- Natural, sustainable material made by laminating strips together
- Made with urea-formaldehyde glues, which outgas after production
- Very hard and durable; some are much harder than oak
- Available in light and dark colors; can be stained

CERAMIC TILE
$$

- Wide assortment of colors and styles available
- Extremely durable
- Available in low- and high-glaze finishes
- Unglazed tiled has to be sealed to resist staining
- Grout needs periodic cleaning and sealing

STONE
$$$

- Many different types of stone flooring available
- Can be strikingly beautiful
- Extremely durable, but hard underfoot
- Polished surfaces are more slippery than "honed" finishes

CONCRETE
$-$$$

- Can be painted or colored when poured new
- Can be stamped to look like tile when poured new
- Very durable, but hard underfoot
- Can be cold underfoot, particularly if there's no insulation underneath

CARPET
$-$$

- Easy to install
- Available in a wide range of patterns, styles, and materials
- Not extremely durable; can show wear in high-traffic areas
- Relatively hard to clean
- Should not be installed in areas that might get wet

WOOD

STONE

Play Spaces

Every house should have place where kids can just be kids, a space all their own, outside of their bedrooms, that reflects their inquisitive, fun-loving nature. Such a play space must accommodate quiet time when children read, use the computer, or solve puzzles, as well as rough play, whether they're wrestling in a pile of pillows or tossing a ball around.

An up-to-date remodeled basement, outfitted with kids in mind, makes a terrific play space. If this space is incorporated into a more extensive basement remodel, the location and layout can be tailored to take the other spaces, and the needs of the kids, into account.

top • With the otherwise intrusive Lally columns disguised as trees and integrated into the floor plan, walking on this playroom's meandering green carpet path is like going for a walk in the woods. The play area itself is clearly defined by the change in flooring and the lowered ceiling that echoes the shape of the flooring. The long built-in bench lets small children look out the window and provides easy-access storage.

right • This cozy play space is separated from the rest of the room by a false beam and a storybook round column. The plush carpet encourages floor activities and the kid-height chalkboard lets budding artists draw to their heart's content.

facing page • To keep the floor clear for boisterous play, the "portable" activity centers are built in along the walls but can swing into action at a moment's notice. A rolling play table is parked in its own "garage" and wheeled storage bins are tucked under a counter. The arts area includes a sliding chalkboard, pinup boards, and a pull-out puppetry panel.

LET ACTIVITIES SHAPE THE PLAN

You can have as much fun creating a playroom as your children will have playing in it. Here is where wild imaginations and whimsical notions are more than just OK. They're desirable. There's someone you can enlist to help you with this scheming: your children. Getting them involved in the planning of their own playroom will give them a sense of pride and ownership. It also offers you an opportunity to connect with your child on a big project. Although there are no hard and fast rules that govern the precise size and shape a playroom should be, following some general guidelines can help make sure that your playroom is a hit.

Although a quick look inside most children's bedrooms might make one think otherwise, kids need a certain amount of structure to feel comfortable and safe. The potential for chaos to reign in a play space can be minimized with proper planning. Begin by listing all the interests and activities that the play space needs to accommodate and group them together in categories. Then map out activity stations, or zones—such as art, kitchen, video/computer, board games, and reading—within the space that match each category. Try to arrange it so that quieter areas are somewhat separated from noisier ones.

Younger children have an out-of-the-way space to play in, but they can still keep an eye on their parents and vice versa. As the children grow this space could be separated with a half-wall of glass panels to keep different-aged kids more separate.

It's helpful to physically define and differentiate the various play-space zones, and that's easy to do in a basement by building a half-wall or low room divider underneath a beam or between two Lally columns. Use the mechanical systems to your advantage by enlisting them to create storage compartments or design details. For instance, lengthen a wall to hide a drainpipe and build some shelving into the recess that's created. Or use a boxed-in duct to add interest to the ceiling and change the flooring materials below it to signal a change of use.

Kids need room to roam, so when planning a play space be sure to leave a good percentage of floor space open. Locate the activity centers, furniture, and storage units around the perimeter of the room as much as possible. Larger items on wheels or caster are easy to move, enabling them to be pushed out of the way. Building tables, desks, and storage into the walls or recesses really opens up floor space.

Break out of the box. Odd shapes, nooks, and alcoves are kid magnets, so look for ways to break the space up. Create alcoves off of the larger space by bumping the playroom into adjacent areas. Children love to have spaces that are scaled to their size, so consider building a secret room under the stairs, where the low ceiling is a perfect fit. Build a platform in an alcove that can serve as a stage or a place to serve tea.

Try to locate the play space so that it has access to a window. If you can't, take a cue from your kids and pretend. Place storage cabinets on either side of a bench, then either paint or build a "garden" window above it and voilà—instant window seat. Of course, kids don't always want to play indoors, so if you have a walk-out basement, or can potentially create one, make sure the playroom has an easy connection to the outside.

top · This kid's size alcove is perfect for curling up with a book, listening to music with headphones, or diving under the pillows for a short nap. Two small square windows take advantage of the above-ground portion of the basement.

left · The low space that's created by the angle of the stairs makes a perfect place to set a table for tea. If people moving up and down the stairs get too intrusive, the partygoers can always duck into the understairs retreat and close the door.

A Playroom for Kids of All Ages

The children who have the run of this basement playroom are probably the envy of the neighborhood. There is plenty of wide-open space for high-energy games, and smaller-scale, out-of-the-way places for quieter activities. The use of triangular cutouts, arched openings, and angled walls adds zip to the quiet color scheme.

Lots of storage—a necessity in a playroom—abounds, from the off-the-shelf storage units around the perimeter of the room to built-ins tucked into the dead space between wall studs.

The wide expanse of floor space allows the space to change as the children grow; it can easily accommodate more furniture for friends who come over to hang out, a Ping-Pong® or pool table, or even the occasional sleepover. The drink and snack center services kids of all ages and is welcome by the parents, who use the adjacent exercise room.

above • Painting the walls of the main space a color similar to that of the rug visually expands the room.

right • It's hard to imagine a better location for a tea-time table. The raised platform puts the windows at the perfect height, and though the ceiling might be too low for adults, it's just right for kids.

facing page • This small space serves as both a play and storage area. A smaller hideaway is tucked under the stairs.

Playroom Safety

A playroom should be a fun but also a safe place to play. Taking some simple precautions can minimize accidents and mishaps.

• Purchase toys that are age-appropriate.

• Check all toys for small parts and remove any small pieces that may pose a choking hazard.

• Use children's furniture that meets the Juvenile Products Manufacturers' Association's certification requirements, and be sure furniture is properly assembled.

• Round over or cover corners on low furniture and counters.

• Attach freestanding furniture securely to a wall to prevent it from tipping over.

• Add safety supports to toy chests with heavy lids to prevent lids from falling on a child's head.

• Ensure that any toy chests can be opened from the inside, so if a child climbs in he or she can get out.

• Use a room monitor to keep tabs on young children while playing.

• Keep blind cords out of the reach of children by either winding them up or tying them near the top of the blind.

top and right · **This rugged wood-paneled wall with fanciful paint hides a kid-size play nook, complete with "window." Kids love their own secret hideaway. When they're grown you can turn it into a closet for out-of-season clothing or other nonessentials.**

above · **Play spaces can be educational as well as fun, as evidenced by this wall mural. Instead of a mural, a plain wall can be covered with burlap or foam panels so that children can hang their artwork.**

FINISHES AND FURNISHINGS

The materials used to finish a playroom, and the stuff that goes into it, are as important as the space itself. They're called on to do double duty. Not only should they create a kid-appropriate atmosphere, but the materials and furnishings also have to be practical, rugged, and easy to clean.

A good place to start is at the bottom, with the floor. Children spend lots of time playing, sitting, or just hanging out on the floor. A good floor is kid-friendly: not too hard, not too cold, and easy to clean. Vinyl, rubber, and other resilient flooring materials are good choices. However, it's better to install them on sleepers or a floating subfloor system. When installed directly on the concrete slab they're anti-child—both hard and cold. Ceramic or clay tile may be easy to clean, but are too hard and cold no matter how they're installed.

Watching a runaway dump truck crash into a vulnerable wall can make you cringe, even if the truck is only a toy. Installing an extrawide baseboard can cut down on the damage. In high-activity areas, or the "tea-time" corner where chairs are pushed away from the table, consider installing wooden wainscoting. For a super-durable wall, replace drywall with cement board.

If you've ever gotten the urge to "decorate" a wide expanse of pristine wall, you know your kids will too. A playroom is the perfect place to give your kids permission to do just that. Cover a section of wall with a chalkboard, dry-erase board, or tile board. Use commercially available "chalkboard paint" to create a chalkboard out of virtually any previously painted wall or other surface. Make king-size pinup boards with cork- or burlap-covered walls where kids can hang up their artwork or make collages. Kids also love to watch themselves in action, so accommodate them by installing a large, unbreakable mirror.

Creating Zones for Multiple Activities

This playroom was designed with the understanding that a structured environment, one that separates out various activities, makes children feel secure and actually encourages creativity. Utilizing the beam, Lally column, and storage divider, this open space is divided into two major zones—one for quiet and the other for more active pursuits.

In the quiet area, a cozy couch is positioned to face the TV, which is located on the opposite wall. However, easy access to books also encourages children to read. Arts and crafts occupy the rest of the playroom. Easy-clean circles clearly mark where the crafts table and easel are supposed to be, and remain.

A simple, subdued color scheme is a good choice for a playroom. With this approach the walls and floors recede into the background, allowing the furnishings, toys, and artwork to take center stage. Although the beige carpet and walls follow that guideline, a surprise— one vibrant wall—ties the space together.

above · Kids love to see how they measure up. This oversize "yardstick" keeps track of their growth, although in no time at all the measuring lines will be marked on the wall.

left · Cylindrical pillows can be used either as extra seating or as part of an impromptu game. The whimsical suspended lamp brightens the mood as well as the room.

facing page · This floor-to-ceiling chalkboard encourages children, no matter their size, to draw to their heart's content. It can be dangerous for young children to climb on chairs, so for safety provide a raised platform or a short, stable ladder to reach the higher sections.

An effective decorating strategy is to create a relatively neutral background with items that are costly or difficult to replace, such as floors and built-ins. Introduce pizzazz with things that can grow with the kids: tables, chairs, and, of course, the toys and activities. Although bold colors are certainly appropriate in a playroom, too much of a good thing can be overwhelming. Painting a wall or two with subdued colors can punch up the brighter ones and make the room feel less cluttered. In some activity centers—a reading nook, for example—quieter colors make sense.

Furnishing a playroom is perhaps the most enjoyable part of creating a play space. Although you want to outfit the playroom with age-appropriate, skill-building furnishings and toys, don't lose sight of practicality. Desks, counters, and cabinets finished with easy-care laminates are colorful and make cleanup a snap. High-gloss paints and tough-skinned polyurethane finishes do the same for wooden chairs and benches.

STORAGE

The way to counteract the tornado effect, where toys are littered everywhere and cover every surface, is to provide ample and appropriate storage. Employing a mix of storage options—drawers, bins, shelves, chests, and cubbies—will ensure that everything will have its proper place. Storage should be easy to use. Sticky drawers or hard-to-open doors can frustrate a child and the toys may end up next to, not in, the storage unit.

Storage should be height-appropriate. For younger children concentrate the storage close to the floor. As the kids grow, taller cabinets and higher shelves can be added. Some toys—such as dolls or stuffed animals—are perfectly at home in open cubbies and shelves, whereas others should be more contained. Clear plastic storage bins not only make it easy for kids to find toys, but when it's cleanup time they can readily find the right place to put the toys away. Corralling waste paper and trash is also important. Strategically placed, brightly colored trash bins will encourage cleanup. Color coding the trash containers will start children thinking about recycling at an early age.

DETAILS THAT WORK

A Bounty of Bins

Putting individual storage bins for toys and supplies on low shelves makes it easy for kids to reach them. Small bins can be carried around, and equipping them with easy-read labels simplifies cleanup time.

above · Clearly intended for athletically minded kids, this large basement rec center allows kids to run off their energy when it's cold or rainy outside. The linoleum floor is easy to clean but more important stands up to the abuse of shoes and sports equipment.

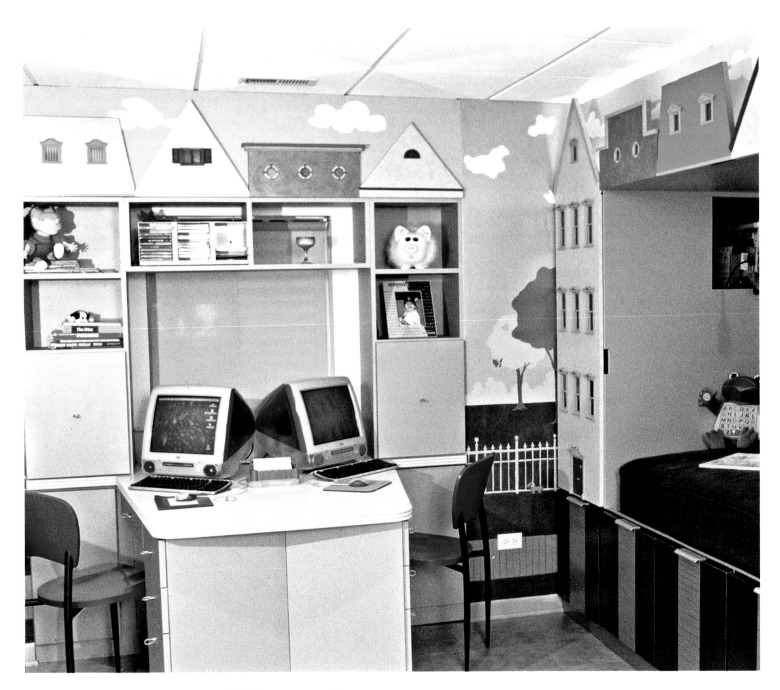

above • A whimsical environment makes even older kids want to stay a bit. "Townhouses" liven up the windowless room and provide a great spot for storage and a computer center. A sleeping bunk is a great addition to the space.

Kids' Storage

Keeping a playroom clean requires the cooperation of two parties: your children and you. Getting children to pick up toys is no easy task to begin with, but if you don't supply adequate and appropriate storage, it's much tougher. Here are some ideas that will help the situation.

1. Closets will hold a lot more toys and games if shelves of different sizes are used. These white melamine types are supported on inexpensive shelf brackets. They can be found at most home stores and are fairly simple to install. 2. Rethink ordinary items to use as storage. This rolling laundry sorter provides perfect storage for odd-shaped items like balls and other sports equipment, and can be wheeled right outside if your basement has a walk-out area. 3. Neatly organized with custom shelving designed for sorting and storing lots of different colored paper, this spacious craft room makes crafting a family affair. The separate table and counter workstations allow child and parent to work on different projects or combine their talents and work together. 4. Although it's utilitarian in nature, storage also has its creative side and can contribute to the overall design of a room. Here the shelving steps back to reveal a pinup board. The shelving on the adjacent wall above the lower cabinet, which echoes the shape of the soffit above, has a sculptural feel.

Craft and Hobby Spaces

If your hobby is relegated to a corner of the dining room table and needs to be picked up daily in order for you to eat, a dedicated space in your new basement could be just what you—and your family—needs.

If you're an experienced crafter, you probably have a good idea of how much space you need. If not, talk to your friends who do the same or similar crafts and visit their spaces to see what works for them. Measure spaces that you really like and sketch out the arrangement of the counters, tables, and other surfaces on graph paper.

It's best to organize craft spaces around activity centers. For example, a sewer's activity list might include areas for machine sewing, cutting, pressing, fitting, and hand finishing. Next to each activity note the dimensions—length, width, and height—of the work surface that's required. Then play around with different arrangements until you find the one that best fits the space and your needs. Generally speaking, L-, T-, and U-shaped spaces are more efficient than straight, in-line workspaces. You might even want to consider a large work island in the middle of the space. Organize storage within the activity centers as well, and utilize a mix of shelves, drawers, and cubbies. Adapt storage from other rooms in the house, such as pull-out trays and spice-jar organizers used in the kitchen.

Not all work surfaces have to be stationary. A rolling table or counter with a drop-down leaf provides flexibility. Be sure to account for the space that's required for machinery and equipment associated with your craft.

Craft spaces need good ambient light, of course, but excellent task lighting is more important. Although task lighting can come from fixed sources—undercabinet lights, for example—moveable lights may be more effective. Adjustable floor lamps are one option. Tensor lamps, like those used by architects and designers, are great for tasks done at a desk or table. Plan ahead when designing the lighting to be sure enough electrical outlets have been included, so that wires don't need to run across the floor.

top • The layout of this project room off a bedroom is an idea that can be applied to any room in the house, particularly in a finished basement. The countertop peninsula provides ample room to see your handiwork from three sides, and storage is located nearby for easy retrieval and cleanup of items used most.

above • Take over one corner of a basement room by installing stock kitchen cabinets found at your local home center. Coupled with a premade countertop, this setup makes a great, simple sewing center.

A Craft Space with Flair

A well-designed craft space should not only be functional but also foster inspirational thinking. This sewing room scores on both accounts. The efficient, in-line work counter provides ample space for layout and stitching. The fabrics are categorized by color and patterns and stored on open shelving, making it easy to see what's in stock and quickly retrieve the appropriate pieces.

Excellent lighting, a basic craft-room requirement, is handled with aplomb. Task lighting, which often takes up counter space or gets in the way, is provided here by unobtrusive downlights. They're installed in an overhead soffit and concealed behind a Plexiglas® lens. Inconspicuous, adjustable recessed ceiling lights illuminate the open shelves and pinup board. A wide chair rail, which separates the space vertically, is used as a handy shallow shelf.

above • This generous pinup board puts information and idea-inspiring material in clear view and gets them up off of the counter, where they can get lost under layers of cloth.

left • Although open to the rest of the basement, this craft space is tucked out of the way. The purple walls create a sense of calm, somewhat offsetting the colorful unkemptness of the open shelves. If more counter space is needed in the future, it can easily be added underneath the windows.

Perhaps music is more your thing and you long for a place for a weekly jam session. The basement is the perfect spot. Although the acoustics might not be at the level of an opera house, the space does lend itself to making noise. Conversely, a basement room can separate you from the hubbub of family life, allowing you to practice that quiet piece undisturbed.

If playing music is an occasional activity that you do with friends or family, you can probably set up in a corner of a larger basement space. But if you're serious about your music and need a dedicated music room, you need to be serious about outfitting it. The most important feature to consider is sound control. Even though it's relatively isolated, appropriate measures must be taken to keep your music in, and extraneous noise out, of your basement room. Money spent on soundproofing techniques is a smart move, so consider using the top-of-the-line sound-isolation measures outlined on p. 142. Remember that most of these measures have to be coordinated with the various phases of construction, so be sure to plan ahead.

Of course, the type of instrument you play, and whether you play alone or with others, influences the space. A baby grand piano or four-piece band is going to need more space than a single guitarist, but you don't want to make the space so small that practicing becomes a claustrophobic event. Although storage needs are minimal, you may need shelves or file cabinets for books, notes, and sheet music.

Good lighting is another important aspect of a music room, but to avoid compromising soundproofing measures be sure to choose the types of fixtures carefully. Instead of installing wall- and ceiling-mounted fixtures, which make holes that need to be sealed, use torchieres or similar floor lamps to create ambient lighting. Task light can also be accomplished with floor lamps or tensor lamps. Avoid recessed lights at all costs, as they are hard to seal for sound.

If you play an electric instrument, with its associated amplifiers and electronic equipment, you should plan for a separate electric circuit and plenty of outlets. Again, when installing outlets be sure to adhere to good sound-isolation measures and do not install outlets in adjacent stud bays.

facing page · You may need nothing more than an out-of-the-way place to strum a guitar and sing quietly to yourself.

left · Ready to rock. This basement space has the look and feel of a nightclub, complete with an elegant bar, raised stage, and mood lighting.

Laundry Rooms

Not too long ago doing the laundry was a task often relegated to a corner of an unfinished basement. Although laundries can be squeezed into tight, closet-size spaces located off of a hall, those arrangements tend to be inefficient and ineffective. Nowadays the laundry room has become a domain unto itself, outfitted with attractive appliances, a drying center, a folding station, an ironing area, and storage compartments.

For many, moving the laundry room near the main living areas is preferred. But if you're planning an extensive remodel that includes a family room, craft room, or home gym, the basement may be just the place for your upgraded laundry room. Even though you'll have to carry the laundry downstairs, you might be able to coordinate doing the wash to coincide with other activities. One major advantage to having the laundry in the basement is that when a hose breaks—and at some point one will—the flood of water that follows doesn't leak through the floor, ruining the ceilings, walls, and floors below it. A basement laundry room can also be combined with a full or half-bath if such an arrangement seems a little awkward in a first-floor bathroom that's used by guests.

Although there's no ideal size or shape, to maximize convenience your laundry room must accommodate several workstations: sorting, soaking and washing, drying and folding, and touch-up and ironing. Arranging the layout so that it coincides with the flow of the task makes the job run more smoothly.

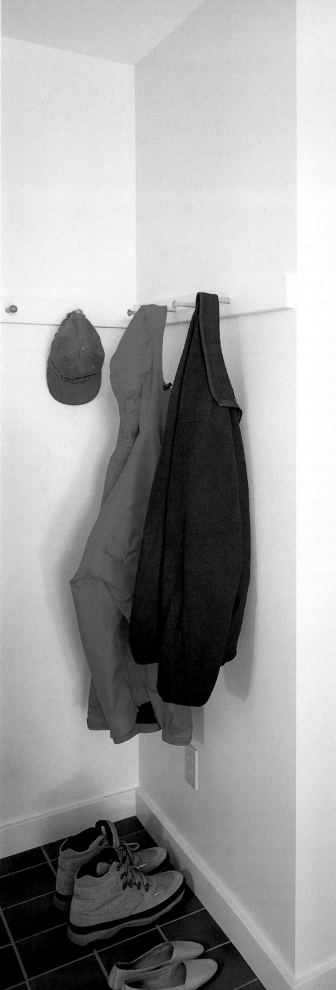

above · Readily available items help to make this laundry area more functional. A stock cabinet/countertop, like those found at most home centers, provides adequate storage for cleaning supplies. Consider easy-to-install wire shelving, like the units here, for stowing beach towels, the dog's leash, or a sewing kit.

left · Located adjacent to an exterior door and part of the mudroom entry, this washer and dryer are conveniently tucked into its own alcove. Louver doors allow air to circulate, helping to keep moisture from building up when they're closed.

facing page · This no-nonsense, hard-working laundry is simple but well outfitted. The large single-bowl sink and the wall-mounted, swing-arm faucet make presoaking even bulky clothes easy. The clothes rack can be used to air-dry damp things or hang ironed clothes.

When planning a laundry room, include a counter that's at least 2 ft. long for sorting clothes. That laundry basket can be stored on an open shelf under the counter until it's needed later. A two-bowl sink, approximately 30 in. wide, for soaking especially dirty or stained clothes and washing delicate items is best located in the counter adjacent to the sorting area. The washer and the drier come next. Side by side they are about 5 ft. wide. Stackable units take up about half that space, but interrupt the flow and should be installed at one end of the counter. Some of the newer washers and driers can be installed under a counter. There are also units that combine washing and drying in one machine.

It's convenient to have a counter next to the drier for folding clean clothes. A clothes rack or bar is handy for hanging up clothes that are removed from the drier before they're completely dry. If your ironing is limited to a quick touch-up of collars and creases you may get away with a small countertop ironing board. Otherwise you might need room for a full-size, freestanding ironing board. As an alternative, an ironing board cabinet is compact, can be installed in a standard 2×4 stud wall, and hides the ironing board neatly behind a door.

Laundry room storage needs are actually pretty basic. Laundry detergents, softeners, soaps, and antistatic sheets can be stored in cabinets or in drawers and roll-out shelves below the counters. If the vacuum cleaner lives in the laundry room, consider installing a tall broom-type cabinet to keep the hoses, cord, and attachments out of the way. The laundry room can also house extra linens and out-of-season blankets. This is particularly helpful if your newly remodeled basement includes a guest room.

right • This full-service laundry center provides plenty of storage and takes advantage of otherwise wasted wall space with the fold-away ironing board and shoe shelves. In addition, the floor underneath the washer/drier is waterproof tile and, in the event of a leak, the tile curb prevents water from ruining the wood floor.

Basic Laundry Needs

There are a number of basic needs that every well-appointed laundry should meet. Some are necessary, whereas others make doing the laundry a bit less of a chore.

Essential Elements

• Washer, which needs hot and cold water supplies and a drain line.

• Electric dryer, which may require a 240v circuit; gas dryer, which requires gas to be piped into the laundry room. Driers must be safely vented to the outside. Metal vent pipes, rather than plastic, are recommended.

• Ample ambient and task lighting, which is particularly important near the ironing board.

Amenities

• Solid-surface countertops, which are impervious to water and last much longer than plastic laminate.

• Resilient flooring, which is easier on the feet.

• Laundry chute from the upper floors; check building codes for requirements or restrictions.

• Built-in speakers for listening to the radio.

• Intercom to children's bedrooms.

• Phone.

above · A stacked washer/drier is a real space saver and in a small room can free up enough counter space to permit the installation of a laundry sink and additional undercounter storage.

PRIVATE

The comings and goings of family life can be disruptive. Close but out of the way, your basement can be converted into a place for quiet work, a refuge from all the hubbub, or a retreat for guests.

SPACES

Home Offices

Working at home is part of many people's lives, whether it's telecommunicating one day a week, running a home business, or simply finishing up work that's brought home from the office. A separate space makes work more efficient, and there's no better place to locate a home office than in a remodeled basement. Not only are construction costs lower than adding on new space, but the impact on family life is minimized. Plus, a basement can provide ample space, privacy, and direct access to the outdoors for visitors and clients.

Building a home office from scratch is a great opportunity to design a space that's customized expressly for you. Although you might not have the money to hire a professional designer, you should allot ample time for planning your office. Think of it as an investment in your business that will enhance your working environment and increase your productivity.

To begin, take into account the type of work you're going to do in your home office. If this space is truly a place of business, your requirements will likely be different than if you just need space to work a few hours a week. The work you do will obviously impact the space you need, but so should your working style. It's also important to think about how your business might grow or change in the future and incorporate those ideas into the initial planning stages.

top · An in-line work area creates a hefty amount of storage space because entire walls can be utilized. The bottom cabinets have a smaller depth to allow for the work surface, whereas the upper two rows of cabinets protrude into the empty space, allowing them to be deeper.

right · This combination home office and family room functions well on a few different levels. When the office is in use, the large desk accommodates multiple people. With clients' chairs facing away from the family room, visitors aren't distracted. When the day is done, the seating area can be used without infringing on the office area.

facing page · This efficient little office space has a lot going for it: windows, a two-workstation floor plan, and plenty of counter space. The doors let light into and out of the space and can be closed to mute noise.

Ready for Work

This spacious, one-person home office appears to be all business. The richly finished, custom-made desk, cabinetry, and bookshelves create a stately atmosphere. The highly polished black stone desktop and geometrically patterned carpet increase the mood. But a quick look at the contents of the bookshelves reveals that even serious business has its lighter side. The long credenza opposite the bookshelves provides ample space for a desktop copier and fax. The credenza, along with the closed-off shelves at the bottom of the bookcase, offers a generous amount of storage.

The owner carefully positioned his desk to take advantage of the office's corner location. The desk commands a view out the window and of the fireplace and TV. Light from two directions is a rarity in a basement room, and the window located behind the desk brightens what would otherwise be a dark corner. Horizontal blinds provide visual privacy while allowing light to enter the room. Cabinetry behind the desk completes what is an efficient and handsome work area.

above and facing page · Attention to detail is evident in this office. The raised-panel treatment on the front of the desk (facing page) is repeated on the wall cabinet behind the desk as well as on the built-in cabinet doors below the TV (above).

left · Wall-washing recessed ceiling lights highlight the items displayed on this custom-built bookcase. Most of the shelves are lined up, adding to the office's orderly atmosphere. Adjustable shelving allows for greater flexibility should the need arise.

PRIVACY AND SOUNDPROOFING

With a solid understanding of your requirements, it's time to shape your lower-level office in a way that will meet those needs. Of prime importance is location. Determine where in the basement makes the most sense to situate the office. If your office is the only finished room in the basement there's much more flexibility, but if other rooms are planned as well, compromises will have to be made.

Separating your office from your family and your family from your work may be important. Of course, locating your office in a corner of the basement and enclosing it with walls and a door creates a private office. If you will see clients or visitors frequently, it's best to have a separate entrance where they can access your office without disturbing your family. A walk-out basement offers the perfect solution. However, it may be necessary to add a new entry door on the first floor or even to build a second set of stairs to the basement.

Another concern may be noise. The sound of feet tromping above your head or the TV blaring two rooms away can be very distracting as you work, and your work might be distracting to others sharing the basement (and even the home in some cases). There are a range of soundproofing techniques to consider. Most are only effective when implemented during construction rather than when applied as a band-aid solution after the fact; be sure to consider the options early on in the design process.

Access to windows may be another point of contention when your office shares the basement. Weigh the pluses—natural light, a view out—against the minuses—loss of privacy and potential distractions. Then decide where the windows are most important: the office or another space, perhaps the family room.

Basic Soundproofing Techniques

To control noise you must deal with two types of sound: airborne noise, which travels through the air in the form of sound waves, and impact-produced noise, such as footsteps, which moves through the structure of a home.

A **basic acoustic treatment** is the simplest, lowest-cost approach:
- Seal all holes, gaps, joints between surfaces, and penetrations in the floor, walls, and ceiling with an acoustical caulk.
- Install sound-control batt insulation in wall cavities.
- Add an acoustical, or "mass-loaded," vinyl sheet over the studs on one side of the wall.
- Use $\frac{5}{8}$-in. drywall instead of $\frac{1}{2}$-in. drywall.
- Install a heavy carpet and pad on the floors above the basement.

Acoustic separation is the next step up and is often used for home theatres. This approach includes all the basic sound-control measures plus some other techniques:
- Seal all holes, gaps, joints between surfaces, and penetrations in the floor, walls, and ceiling with an acoustical caulk.
- Install sound-control batt insulation in wall cavities.
- Add an acoustical, or "mass-loaded," vinyl sheet over the studs on one side of the wall.
- Use $\frac{5}{8}$-in. drywall instead of $\frac{1}{2}$-in. drywall.
- Install a heavy carpet and pad on the floors above the basement.
- Add a layer of special "impact-loaded" vinyl sheet on walls and ceilings.
- Build walls with staggered, offset studs—typical 2×4 studs installed with 2×6 top and bottom plates.

Acoustic isolation is the most expensive method and is used in high-end projects or when near total sound control is required. It includes all the basic methods plus a decoupling technique:
- Seal all holes, gaps, joints between surfaces, and penetrations in the floor, walls, and ceiling with an acoustical caulk.
- Install sound-control batt insulation in wall cavities.
- Add an acoustical, or "mass-loaded," vinyl sheet over the studs on one side of the wall.
- Use $\frac{5}{8}$-in. drywall instead of $\frac{1}{2}$-in. drywall.
- Install a heavy carpet and pad on the floors above the basement.
- Use spring or rubber-type isolators that completely separate the finished wall and ceiling material from the structural members.

left · Placing the computer screen at a diagonal not only creates an efficient work triangle, with work and storage areas on either side, but also shifts the line of sight. Rather staring at the wall directly ahead, the person using the computer has longer, more interesting views across the counter toward the corner of the room.

bottom left and right · This modest open-plan workspace is separated from the other basement spaces by half-walls that were built just high enough to conceal the desks behind them. Although there is ample room for two workstations, storage is limited. The two wall-hung cabinets are installed too high to be reached easily. The space is also lacking personality and would benefit by dressing up the bare walls with photos or paintings.

PLANNING THE LAYOUT

With the location of the office set, turn your attention to the size, shape, and interior layout. As you design the space, think about the layout creatively—it doesn't necessarily have to be a square or rectangle. Basements often have odd shapes and nooks and crannies, which can make ideal places for equipment, storage, or a coffee maker, so use these to your advantage and plan them into the design right from the beginning.

Of course, the optimal size and shape of your office is largely determined by the size, shape, and number of desks and surfaces your work and associated equipment requires. It also will be influenced by whether you work alone or will have to accommodate another person. To help you decide what kind of workstation setups and furniture arrangements will work best, consider experimenting with a low-cost computer program. Alternately, make some paper cutouts and push them around on a floor plan drawn on graph paper. Don't forget to include a second workstation for the bookkeeper, if necessary, and a comfortable seating area or conference table for talks or meetings with clients. Think, too, about the need for a coffee or snack station and where that would be best located.

Money to set up a home office can be in short supply. To get the most out of limited funds, set up a strict budget that includes both constructing and furnishing your office and stick to it. However, it can be cost effective to splurge on those things that are difficult or costly to replace, such as walls, floor, and ceiling structures, and save on items that can easily be upgraded, such as furniture.

above · Uncluttered white space means there's nothing to get between you and your work.

facing page · This office features two distinct areas. The counter, which is higher than the standard 30-in. desk height, is used for meeting with clients when reviewing plans and other documents. A sitting area is used as both waiting room and open "conference" area.

Three Typical Office Configurations

When creating a home office, you want it to be both functional and organized yet also let your personality and personal preferences come through. Although the best perk of having a home office is that you can reconfigure it to meet your changing needs, it's best to look at office layouts that work and adapt one as a starting point.

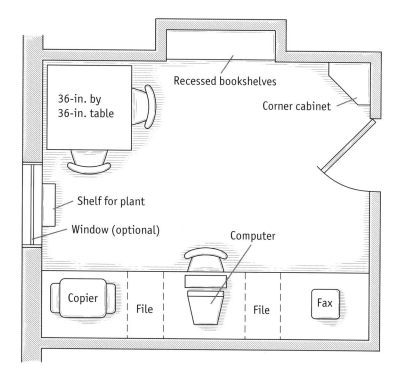

Small Office— 11 ft. by 12 ft.

This single-wall layout is economical and efficient, yet provides ample workspace and storage. The 3-ft.-sq. table can be used for additional workspace or pulled away from the wall to accommodate a four-person conference.

No matter how large or small your office area, a built-in desk with shelves and drawers all around makes the most of wall space.

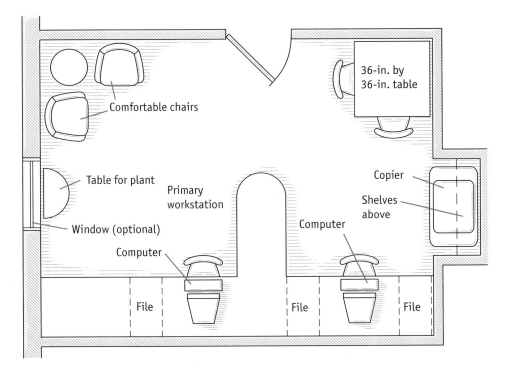

Comfortable chairs

36-in. by
36-in. table

Copier

Table for plant

Primary
workstation

Shelves
above

Window (optional)

Computer

Computer

File

File

File

Medium Office—
12 ft. by 16 ft.

This "T" arrangement creates two separate workstations, making the most of the larger floor plan. A comfortable seating group is tucked in one corner and, to save space, the copier is recessed into an alcove.

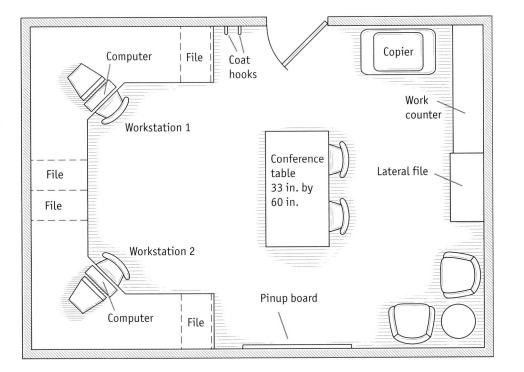

Computer

File

Coat
hooks

Copier

Work
counter

Workstation 1

File

File

Conference
table
33 in. by
60 in.

Lateral file

Workstation 2

Computer

File

Pinup board

Large Office—
14 ft. by 20 ft.

Two people can work together comfortably in this large office. Both workstations have ample surface area and access to files.

STORAGE

The need for adequate storage space also shapes your office. The mountains of supplies that are an essential part of any office can get out of control. A mix of file drawers, wall-mounted shelves and cabinets, and built-in closets will put everything in its place.

Storage units can be intrusive, so if space is tight consider recessing them into a wall or bumping them into an adjacent space. Here's a good opportunity to use those odd-shaped spaces to best advantage. Consider pullout storage drawers under the stairs, or add a half-wall between Lally columns to house bookshelves on the bottom and an expansive counter on top. Remember that it's not necessary to store everything right in the office; in fact, it's sometimes even better not to. Extra supplies and outdated files can be kept in another space—perhaps a large walk-in closet. However, to prevent damage to stored items from excess moisture, any storage space should be air-conditioned or ventilated.

DETAILS THAT WORK

Compact yet Complete

A small, round undermount bar sink makes wiping down this granite counter an easy task. Room for a coffee maker, an undercounter refrigerator, and plenty of storage for dishware complete this well-appointed snack center.

ADDING CREATURE COMFORTS

You are going to inhabit your office, not just work there, so be sure to create an enjoyable environment. A comfortable chair and an ergonomic primary workstation are indispensable. Even if you're on a tight budget, don't skimp here.

During the course of the workday you're going to get thirsty or hungry. Going upstairs to the kitchen can break your concentration—the kids will want help with something or your spouse might start asking about plans for the evening. To avoid these distractions, build a drink/snack center into your office. It can be simple: an undercounter refrigerator, a coffee maker, a microwave, and storage for dishware. The same is true for the bathroom. Plan a half-bath close to the office.

Maintaining healthy air quality with adequate ventilation, air conditioning, and dehumidification is essential for a successful home office. Lights and electrical equipment generate a lot of heat and can easily overheat the relatively small space of a home office. When discussing mechanical systems with the installer, be sure to alert him or her if you use glues or solvents. Oversizing the systems may be prudent.

left · There's more to this simple bill-paying area than is first apparent. The custom-built cabinetry includes ample drawer space, open shelving, plus some lateral files. A section of the counter is lower to put the computer keyboard at the proper height. Hopefully the bill paying goes quickly, because the wooden chair looks less than comfortable.

facing page · These bookshelves are only part of a larger library and the small desk intended to be used for some serious reading. Instead of being pushed right up against the wall, the desk is positioned so that it's at the proper distance for the reader to look up and enjoy the art hanging on the wall.

WIRE FOR FUTURE INFRASTRUCTURE

Even a carefully thought-out design can't account for every eventuality, so it's helpful to plan flexibility into your office. Generally, this means the ability to rearrange the furniture to correspond with changing needs. A major limiting factor is a poorly planned infrastructure; namely, the wiring.

Office equipment draws a lot of juice. There are better ways to get exercise than running back and forth to the electrical panel to reset a thrown circuit breaker. It's a good idea to run at least one separate circuit that's totally dedicated to your office. If your home has only 100-amp service, it should probably be upgraded to 200 amps.

During the framing of your office have the electrician wire walls to accommodate every type of wire you might need. It seems like there's never enough electrical outlets to go around, so be excessive and put a lot of them on every wall. Also, have at least two phone lines installed. A professional, efficient home office must have separate home and business lines. If you'll need a dedicated fax line, add one now as well.

A well-lit room is obviously a must, but properly designed lighting can also enhance flexibility. Use indirect ceiling fixtures or cove lighting for ambient lighting. Ordinarily, wall sconces are a good choice for indirect lighting, but in an office they take up valuable wall space and may be in the way as the layout changes. Desk-mounted lamps or floor lamps provide adjustable task lighting. This is where all those extra electrical receptacles come in. They allow the task lights to be plugged in close to a desk or work surface without the need for extension cords. Track lighting is perfect for lighting photos and artwork. The light heads can be slid along the track to keep up with rearranged wall hangings.

above · Regardless of how large your office space is, be sure there's plenty of storage. This informal space utilizes open shelving, which is easy to access but can instantly look cluttered. Smaller boxes, baskets, and desk accessories help to keep the space organized.

facing page top · To open up the taller floor space, this wall-to-wall built-in is appropriately located under a low soffit and provides a seemingly endless amount of shelf and storage space. The deeper center section breaks up the long array and visually separates the desk and seating areas of this long and narrow study.

facing page bottom · Table lamps are a good choice for creating task lighting on desks. They can be moved to where light is needed. Available in many styles, it's easy to choose one to blend with any décor.

Lighting

All too often decisions about lighting are left to the last minute, when it's too late to add built-in lighting, making locating lighting fixtures just an afterthought. Planning out a lighting scheme for a basement is particularly important given the reduced impact of natural lighting on the space. Style and size of fixtures can make or break a space, so invest wisely.

1. An adjustable recessed light was carefully centered on the fireplace during the rough framing, positioned to highlight the painting hung above the mantel. Recessed lights located along the adjacent wall do the same for the wall-hung artwork. 2. Overhead lighting can cast shadows on stairs, potentially creating a dangerous situation. These small, wall-mounted downlights brightly illuminate the stair treads, making it easy to see the way down. 3. Whimsy best describes this sitting area for two. The shallow alcove begins to define the space, but it's the lighting that carries the day. Low-voltage track lighting combines adjustable fixtures, which bring a warm glow to the lemon-yellow walls, with fanciful pendant lights that illuminate the area around the chairs. The glass stem and shade of the table lamp complete the setting. 4. With track lighting, multiple fixtures can be trained on the same object, creating even light and eliminating shadows. 5. The adjustable arms give this lamp a sculptural look, but they are also practical and can be adjusted to provide perfect light for reading. If placed between a pair of chairs, it can serve two readers.

Studies

The racket of preparing meals and cleaning up afterward. The blare of the TV or video games. The clatter of children's feet. If you're feeling the need for a private space all your own— someplace where you can get away from it all—a basement study may be just right for you.

As you dream about your own special place, think about what you'd like to have: perhaps a quiet retreat to read and write uninterrupted, a cozy space where you can put your feet up and listen to your favorite music, or somewhere to knit a sweater or play chess against the computer in complete peace. Although all these activities can certainly be done in a living room or family room, it's just not the same. Besides, with a separate study you can do some midnight reading without disturbing your spouse.

Although it might be tempting to combine a study with a home office space, it's probably a temptation to avoid. Although it certainly makes sense to pay the family bills in a study, being surrounded by an office environment is not exactly conducive to relaxing. So go ahead, spoil yourself. Create your own, separate study. You deserve it.

EXPRESS YOUR PERSONALITY

Your study is all about you—what you want and what you like—so it's the perfect opportunity to create a space that expresses your personality. Surround yourself with the things that you cherish, that evoke fond memories, and that speak to your inner self. But first come some practical considerations.

One of the advantages of building a study is that unless you have some very specific needs there is no set size or shape a study must be. So be creative when seeking out a place for your private space and don't turn your back on the odd-shaped nooks and crannies that are common in basements. Even though you will almost certainly enclose your study with walls and a tight-fitting door, if possible, it's best to locate a study away from other basement rooms, such as family or game rooms.

above • The richly detailed fireplace surround, built-in cabinetry, and ceiling beams create a refined atmosphere that's perfect for quiet reading or serious conversation with friends. The light-colored carpet and white sections of wall contrast with dark woodwork, preventing what otherwise might be a feeling of somber surroundings.

facing page top • This special study is hidden away behind an elegant pair of doors. The tile floor leads right up the stairs to the carpeted space.

facing page bottom • Don't have the space for a full-blown reading room but need a place to get away? Build in a window seat (even without the window) that includes a soft cushion, lots of pillows, and a storage drawer for blankets and other essentials needed to keep you cozy while curling up with a good book.

Locating a study so it has a window can be a plus or a minus, depending on your needs. If you really find it relaxing to sit and daydream while looking out a window, a window is a high priority. On the other hand, windows can compromise privacy, so a windowless location in the basement may be perfect. Also, books and some collectibles are damaged by natural light, so they won't miss a window.

Outfit your study to accommodate the things that will populate it. Books, naturally, are common in studies, so be sure to include plenty of built-in or freestanding bookshelves. Unless you have a large book collection, however, don't get carried away and fill the entire space with shelving. If you have collections of small items, shallow shelves can be built right into 2×4 walls.

top • Supported by L brackets screwed into the studs, these simple shelves are easy to install on just about any wall. Of course, to stand the books on end would require heavy book ends or a type that can clip on to the ends.

right • If you have a large collection of books but limited space in your study for shelving, look to places that are nearby for help. These shelves maximize the available space, and you might even find yourself sitting and reading on the stairs.

above • Cozy up to the fire, sink back into the cushioned chair, read a book, or just gaze absentmindedly into the flames. The warm wood Arts and Crafts style fireplace surround gives this corner retreat a sense of place and makes one wonder: Was it inspired by the chair or was the chair chosen because it matched perfectly?

Think carefully about whether or not you want a TV or stereo system in your study. If your study is truly a retreat you might consider the daring step of banning the phone. Including a small snack and drink center, or even just a small refrigerator, means that you can hide out in your study for hours at a time.

How you finish the space establishes the atmosphere and says a lot about yourself. Choose a color scheme that will enhance the mood you want to create. Whites are especially comforting, cooling, and uncomplicated; pastels feel soothing and may conjure up feelings of childhood. If you're a serious reader, try navy blue, dark browns, dark greens, and burgundy. On the other hand, bright cheery colors may be for you. Ceiling beams wrapped with woodwork blend well with heavy casings and baseboards and add to a sense of security and calm. False beams can be installed to create a desired pattern.

Guest Rooms

When you first moved into your house, chances are you had a spare bedroom that was immediately designated as the guest room. As you lived in the house, perhaps you found that you needed a little space to set up your sewing machine. A corner of this room worked just fine, although it was a bit inconvenient to put things away every time you had an overnight guest. The kids got older and demanded their own rooms. Out went the sewing and the walls of that "spare" room were now covered with pop-star posters—the guests were relegated to the pull-out sleeper in the family room.

For people who like to entertain house guests, this situation is, of course, untenable. Even if overnight visitors are infrequent, without an appropriate space for them to stay their brief presence can be disruptive to you and uncomfortable for them. And, of course, there's always a chance that in the event of an emergency a family member or close friend may need to stay with you for an extended period. Creating a new guest room in the basement will let you be truly welcoming the next time an old friend drops by unannounced.

right · Basement windows that are high off the floor are usually considered a disadvantage, but here that shortcoming is turned into a positive. Placing the twin beds, complete with headboards, on the outside wall makes for an efficient furniture layout.

facing page top · Painting the bathroom a darker shade of blue and using the same border at the top of the wall (not shown) integrates it with the bedroom, making the two rooms feel like a suite.

facing page bottom · Thoughtful planning incorporated two typical basement obstructions into the floor plan. The electrical panel is hidden behind a short built-out section of wall that creates a small display shelf and a place to anchor the queen-size sleigh bed. The boxed-in duct work is located above the bed, where the reduced headroom is less of an issue.

Although there are several advantages to building a basement guest room—lower cost, design flexibility, and built-in privacy, for example—there are two drawbacks you should be aware of as you begin to plan. Accessibility is the first. For someone who has trouble negotiating stairs, the basement is a less than desirable location for a guest room, although it is possible to install a stair lift.

The other issue is isolation. Although it's true that your guests will want some privacy, and vice versa, if the guest room is the only finished space in the basement your guests might feel like they've been banished to a dungeon. A basement guest room will be more successful if it's planned in conjunction with some other spaces, such as an exercise space, family room, or home office. On the other hand, if you have a live-in nanny or health care provider it's certainly possible that you might want to turn most, if not all, of the basement into guest quarters.

DETERMINE THE ROOM SIZE

There probably is enough room in your basement for a generous-size guestroom, so availability of space shouldn't be a much of a factor. Rather, it's the guests themselves who have more of an influence on the size of the guestroom. Are your overnight guests typically friends or family? How many? Are there any children? Are pets welcome?

Although it's impossible to plan for every contingency, a well-thought-out guest room should be able to handle most situations. If you have the space, consider enlarging the guest room to include a separate sitting area with a couple of upholstered chairs and a small table or two.

Another major factor when determining the size of the guest room is, not surprisingly, the size of the bed. Even if you usually have only one guest at a time, planning a guest room with a single bed is too shortsighted. A double bed is better, a queen-size bed generous. Of course, there has to be room to walk around the bed, so it's best to position the bed in the room so that there's enough clearance to walk on both sides. It's easier to make the bed and your guests won't have to climb over each other to get out of bed. A well-appointed guest room also has some other pieces of furniture—dressers, chairs, tables—that need to be accounted for when planning room size.

Accommodating both parents and children in a guest room can be a challenge. If there's a family room in the basement you may be able to skirt the issue by having a sleeper couch where the children can sleep. Another solution is to bump out a small alcove off of the guest room and install a bunk bed behind a curtain. Providing enough space for an inflatable mattress or a fold-up crib for an infant are other possibilities.

Choose the Right Size Bed for Your Needs

Twin, also known as Single

• Overall dimensions: 39 in. wide and 75 in. long

• Width per person: 39 in.

• Twin beds often have a "trundle bed" underneath them to accommodate more than one guest

• Pros: Fit into small rooms; twin sheets are the least costly and available in a wide range of patterns and colors; easy to make

• Cons: May be too short for some people

Double, also known as Full

• Only 15 in. wider than twin, so when sleeping two offers less sleeping space per person than a single

• Overall dimensions: 54 in. wide and 75 in. long

• Width per person: 27 in.

• Pros: Fit into smaller rooms; sheets are less costly than queen or king; relatively easy to make; ample room for a single shorter person

• Cons: May be too short for some people and feel too cramped for two

Queen

• Although 21 in. wider than twin, still offers less sleeping space per person for two people than single beds

• Overall dimensions: 60 in. wide and 80 in. long

• Width per person: 30 in.

• Pros: Extra length means it fits most people; bedding is easy to find and less expensive than king size; fits in average size rooms

• Cons: May be too narrow for large people; some bedding sold as full/queen doesn't fit either size very well

Standard King, also known as Eastern King

• About 18 in. wider than queen and the same length; sold with two half-size box springs or frames and one mattress

• Overall dimensions: 76 in. wide and 80 in. long

• Width per person: 38 in.

• Pros: Most comfortable for two; length is sufficient for most people

• Cons: May be difficult to get into some spaces; won't fit in small rooms; bedding is relatively expensive

left • Even small guest rooms should be outfitted with the minimum—a bed, of course, but also end table and lamp. Small spaces benefit from a simple decorating scheme to help keep the space restful.

facing page top • Tucked under the sheltering lower portion of the ceiling, this guest space is open to the rest of the basement but out of the way. A portable screen, sliding doors, or curtains would provide more privacy and probably be appreciated by most guests.

facing page bottom • The simple touch of putting a chair, particularly a comfortable upholstered one, in a guest room goes a long way. It can be used as temporary clothes "hangers," and, of course, when paired with a lamp, provide a place to read or sew on a button.

Bathrooms

Whether built in conjunction with a family room, home gym, or guest room, a bathroom is an important part of a successful basement remodeling project; not only for the convenience factor, but also as a way to pamper yourself or your guests. Although, of course, the standard three-fixture bathroom—sink, shower/tub, and toilet—is a reasonable choice, you may want to take this opportunity to make this "extra" bathroom a little special. Remember, you don't have to worry about the extra weight of a water-filled tub or water sloshing over the top of the tub or spraying out of the shower. The concrete floor can take it.

1. Under-mount sinks don't have a rim, providing a sleek look and making the countertop easy to clean. 2. Although this sink is installed in a countertop, it has the open look of a pedestal sink and retains the convenience of a vanity. The narrow counter to either side of the sink and the shallow drawer and shelves below provide ample space for toiletries and towels.

3. Narrow, deep shelves are awkward to use, but installing a shower instead of a tub in this bathroom made these shelves wider and more functional. The wide shelving, along with the diagonally laid tile floor, make the room appear bigger. 4. The classic black and white checkerboard floor, simple drawer pulls, and white-painted woodwork give this small bathroom an informal, country feeling. An angled configuration makes it possible to install the shower in a corner and still use the adjacent walls.

Raising the Ceiling to Add Light and Views

Before it was remodeled, this basement had ceilings that were less than 7 ft. high, making it uninhabitable. Not surprisingly, it had only a few small windows and two narrow exterior doors. During the remodeling process, virtually the entire existing concrete slab was removed, along with a foot of earth, resulting in a legal and comfortable ceiling height. This not only added 1,100 sq. ft. of valuable new living space, but also opened up the basement to the outside.

To take advantage of the southern exposure and a great view of the nearby reservoir, the tiny windows and doors were replaced by full-height French doors flanked by wide sidelights. As a result, daylight floods the once-dark space and is dispersed by the light-colored walls and glossy-finished engineered oak flooring.

top · This custom-tiled shower continues the color theme begun in the bedroom. The glass shower doors and enclosure expand the bathroom. The simple hook on the back of the door provides a convenient place to hang a towel.

right · The soft bench is a great place for a guest to put a suitcase while unpacking or to sit down while putting on socks and shoes.

above • To work with the floor plan, the closet had to be bumped into the bedroom. Although losing the floor space might be viewed as a problem, the closet actually adds to the room by creating an alcove for the bed and a defined place for the dresser.

To help you visualize how big your guest room might be, take a tape measure into one of your existing bedrooms and measure the bed and all the other furniture. Using these measurements as a guide, continue your planning with graph paper and paper cutouts of the furniture. Play with different arrangements and room shapes until you find the one that works best.

Planning a guest room to minimize the disruptions that guests can cause will make everybody's experience more enjoyable. A door that leads directly outside from the basement allows someone to slip out unnoticed for an early morning jog and gives your guests a bit of independence. It's also important to limit the impact your daily life will have on your guests. If the guest room is below a noisy space like the kitchen, incorporate soundproofing techniques into the structure.

Easy access to a bathroom is a must. A bathroom should be located near, preferably adjacent to, the guest room. If at all possible, build a full bath, particularly if there's only a half-bath on the first floor. It's much more convenient and further reduces potential disruptions. Stock the bathroom with some of the essentials—toothpaste, soap, and other toiletries—that your guests might forget.

FURNISHINGS

When outfitting a guest room, put yourself in your guests' shoes or imagine that you're staying at a fine bed and breakfast. The most important piece of furniture is, of course, the bed. Don't skimp here. Purchase the best-quality mattress your money can buy. If you can't afford a whole new sleep set, consider a high-quality futon or an air mattress on top of an existing box spring.

You don't want your guests living out of suitcases, so provide an ample mix of storage space: a chest of drawers or two, open shelving, and hanging space. A good-size closet is a big plus, but if one can't be designed as part of the room a freestanding armoire can work just as well. Make sure to include hangers.

To help your guests feel at home, nestle a comfortable chair or two and a small coffee table in a corner where they can sit and read or sip a cold drink. To ensure adequate reading light, provide an adjustable floor lamp for each chair. A bookshelf located nearby stocked with a few novels or classics completes the cozy space. Another piece of furniture to consider is a small desk stocked with pens and paper.

above · In addition to a corner sitting area and sumptuous color-coordinating bedding, this bedroom provides direct access to a sun-filled patio. Easy-to-close drapes add a spot of color and just the right amount of privacy.

left · Things aren't always what they appear to be. This floor-to-ceiling built-in storage wall holds a secret. Although the lower drawers are really drawers, the upper ones camouflage three doors that open to reveal an efficient arrangement for hanging clothes.

facing page · This alcove is a perfect place for kids to sleep, whether napping or having a special sleepover. The curtain gives visual privacy and doesn't take up the space needed for doors.

Home Away from Home

Quite naturally, the purpose of most guest rooms is to provide a place for your guests to sleep. But if your guests stay for more that a few days that guest room might begin to feel like a motel room. An adult child that's home for the holidays or house sitting while you go on vacation might have outgrown their childhood bedroom. With a little creative planning, instead of just making a guest room you can turn your basement space into a generous suite, a home away from home.

Instead of letting the bed dominate the room, most of this guest space is given over to a large sitting area, making it feel more like a living room than a guest room. This creates a homey atmosphere and might even encourage your guests to invite you "over" for an evening of conversation.

above · The comforter, extra blankets, and fluffy pillows create a cozy atmosphere. Tight quarters and corner placement of the bed, however, make it difficult to make the bed.

left · A latticework screen separates the bed from the conversation grouping in this guest room suite. The off-white and grey tones of the walls and tile provide a perfect background for the rich browns of the baskets and leather seating.

facing page · Using the same floor tile and color scheme coordinates the bathroom with the rest of the space. In a nice touch, the wainscoting is topped with the same accent tile that runs through the guest room floor. A shelf, counter, or cabinet for toiletries would improve the bathroom.

Window Treatments

Even though there may be few of them, when it comes to dressing them up, basement windows deserve as much attention, if not more, as the windows in the upper-level rooms. Window treatments, such as blinds and shades, not only add to a room's décor; they also control light and create privacy.

1. This floral-patterned Roman shade and nicely detailed curtain rod add a decorative touch to the space. The shade can be raised and lowered with cords that are hidden behind the shade. 2. Basement windows that are high on a wall allow people on the outside to look in, creating a fish-bowl effect. Horizontal blinds can be adjusted to block the view while allowing some light to enter the space. Of course, closing them all the way makes for complete privacy. 3. The combination of blinds and shades gives this home theatre space multiple options. The blinds can be closet for privacy and shut out most of the light. Drawing the floor-to-ceiling curtains blocks out all the daylight and adds to the theater-like atmosphere.

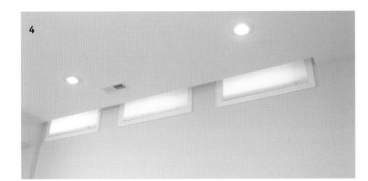

4. A clever bit of framing permitted the installation of some windows, even though they're small, in a space that would have otherwise been windowless. The joist closest to the exterior wall was removed and three small windows were cut into the perimeter "band joist" located directly under the first floor wall. **5.** Shades or blinds that operate from the bottom up are becoming increasingly popular. When partially raised they not only block the view in, but also screen a less than appealing view out. Many of these window treatments can be opened from the top or the bottom.

Periodicals

FINE HOMEBUILDING MAGAZINE
www.taunton.com
Timeless magazine that covers all
aspects of residential design and
construction

ENVIRONMENTAL BUILDING NEWS
BuildingGreen, Inc.
A monthly newsletter featuring
comprehensive information on
a wide range of topics related to
sustainable building, including
energy efficiency, recycled-content
materials, and indoor air quality

THIS OLD HOUSE MAGAZINE
www.thisoldhouse.com
Information about remodeling and
renovating older homes

Books

GREEN BUILDING PRODUCTS
BuildingGreen, Inc.
Features over 1,500 green building
products

INSIDE THE NOT SO BIG HOUSE
Sarah Susanka and Marc Vassallo
The Taunton Press
Takes a close-up look at details and
finishes that make a home special

NEW BUILT-INS IDEA BOOK
Sandor Nagyszalanczy
The Taunton Press
Offers a wealth of ideas for
incorporating built-ins in any room
of the house

Informational Websites

**AMERICAN SOCIETY OF HOME
INSPECTORS**
www.ashi.org
Members offer comprehensive
home inspections and evaluations

BUILDINGGREEN, INC.
www.buildinggreen.com
An independent organization that
provides green building-product
information and publications

BUILDING SCIENCE CORP.
www.buildingscience.com
A consulting company providing
information and homeowner sources
about building technology

ENERGY STAR
www.energystar.gov
Information on energy-efficient
building materials, techniques, and
appliances

U.S. DEPARTMENT OF ENERGY
www.eere.energy.gov/buildings
Comprehensive energy efficiency
and renewable energy information

**U.S. ENVIRONMENTAL
PROTECTION AGENCY**
www.epa.gov
Information on a wide range of
consumer environmental and health
concerns

Professional Organizations

**AMERICAN INSTITUTE OF
ARCHITECTS**
www.aia.org
Lists AIA member architects who
specialize in residential work

**AMERICAN INSTITUTE OF
BUILDING DESIGNERS**
www.aibd.org
Provides professional certification
and member referrals

**AMERICAN SOCIETY OF INTERIOR
DESIGNERS**
www.asid.org
Lists ASID members who work with
residential clients

**NATIONAL ASSOCIATION OF HOME
BUILDERS**
www.nahb.org
Provides member referrals and
information for the homeowner
about remodeling

**NATIONAL ASSOCIATION OF THE
REMODELING INDUSTRY**
www.nari.org
Provides member referrals and
information for the homeowner
about remodeling

**NATIONAL KITCHEN AND BATH
ASSOCIATION**
www.nkba.org
Provides member referrals and
information about kitchen and bath
design

Product Sources

**AMERICAN LIGHTING
ASSOCIATION**
www.americanlightingassoc.com
A trade association that represents
the lighting industry; members
include lighting and fan
manufacturers, retail showrooms,
and lighting designers; provides
consumer information about
lighting

**ASSOCIATION OF THE WALL AND
CEILING INDUSTRY**
www.awci.org
Provides links to its membership,
which includes over 2,000 wall and
ceiling product manufacturers and
distributors

BASEMENT SYSTEMS, INC.
www.basementsystems.com
A network of dealers that provides
basement remodeling consulting,
proprietary products, and equipment

**DRICORE DIVISION, LONGLAC
WOOD INDUSTRIES**
www.dricore.com
Manufacturers of a subfloor panel
system that integrates a water-
resistant polyethylene membrane
with an engineered wood surface

GLOBAL SOURCES
www.globalsources.com
An online supplier of consumer
products, home décor items, and
information

**NATIONAL ASSOCIATION OF
FLOOR COVERING DISTRIBUTORS**
www.nafcd.org
An organization of flooring
manufacturers and distributors
that offers links to other flooring
associations that provide consumer
information and dealer locations

**WINDOW AND DOOR
MANUFACTURERS ASSOCIATION**
www.wdma.com
Lists over 145 manufacturers of
windows and doors

CAD Programs

GOOGLE SKETCHUP
www.sketchup.com
Computer design program capable
of creating 3D drawings, available
in a free downloadable version for
private use or a professional version

**BETTER HOMES AND GARDENS
HOME DESIGNER AND
BETTER HOMES AND GARDENS
INTERIOR DESIGNER**
Two in a series of computer
programs designed with the
homeowner in mind and capable of
doing 3D drawings

CREDITS

p. i: Photo courtesy Owens-Corning Basement Finishing System

p. ii: Photo © Alise O'Brien Photography

p. iv: Photos (left to right) © Steve Vierra Photography, © Jessie Walker Associates, © Eric Roth Photography, © Eric Roth Photography, © Grey Crawford

p. v: Photo © Olson Photographic LLC

p. 1: Photo © Eric Roth Photography

p. 2: (top) Photos (left to right) © Mark Lohman Photography, © Jessie Walker Associates, © Ken Gutmaker, © Anne Gummerson Photography, © Jessie Walker Associates; (bottom) Photo © Jessie Walker Associates

p. 3: Photo © Ken Gutmaker

Ch. 1

p. 4: Photo © Jessie Walker Associates

p. 7: (top) Photo © Gary Easter PHOTOgraphics; (bottom) Photo © David Schrock, Basement Spaces, Inc.; (left) Photo © Mark Lohman Photography

p. 8: Photo © Randy O'Rourke

p. 9: Photo © Jessie Walker Associates

p. 10: Photo © Eric Roth Photography

p. 11: (left) Photo: © Eric Roth Photography; (top & bottom right) Photos © David Schrock, Basement Spaces, Inc.

p. 12: Photo © Eric Roth Photography

p. 13: Photo © Mark Lohman Photography

pp. 14–15: Photos © Sylvain Côté, Absolute Remodeling, Inc

p. 16: Photo © David Schrock, Basement Spaces, Inc.

p. 17 (top) Photo © Tim Lee Photography; (bottom) Photo © Alise O'Brien Photography

p. 18 Photo © Eric Roth Photography

p. 19: (top) Photo © Eric Roth Photography; (bottom) Photo © Ken Gutmaker

p. 20: (left) Photo © Roger Turk, Northlight Photography, Inc.; (right) Photo © David Schrock, Basement Spaces, Inc.

p. 21: (left) Photo © Lee Anne White Photography; (top right) Photo © Todd Caverly; (bottom right) Photo © Jessie Walker Associates

p. 23: (right) Photo © Mark Samu, Samu Studios, Inc.; (left) Photo © Mark Lohman Photography

p. 24: (top) Photo courtesy Owens-Corning Basement Finishing System; (bottom) Photo © Tim Street-Porter

p. 25: Photo © Olson Photographic, LLC

p. 26: Photo © Jessie Walker Associates

p. 28: (top) Photo © Sylvain Côté, Absolute Remodeling, Inc.; (bottom) Photo © Carolyn I. Bates Photography

pp. 30–31: Photos © Sylvain Côté, Absolute Remodeling, Inc.

Ch. 2

p. 32: Photo © Mark Lohman Photography

p. 34: (top) Photo © Steve Vierra Photography; (bottom) Photo © Olson Photographic

p. 35: (top) Photo © Roger Turk, Northlight Photography

p. 36: (top) Photo © Eric Roth Photography; (bottom) Photo © Carolyn I. Bates Photography

p. 37: Photo © Mark Samu, Samu Studios, Inc.

p. 38: Photos © Sylvain Côté, Absolute Remodeling, Inc.

p. 39: (top right & bottom) Photos © Todd Caverly; (top left) Photo © Tria Giovan

p. 40: Photos © Eric Roth Photography

p. 41: Photo © Eric Roth Photography

p. 42: Photo © Mark Samu, Samu Studios, Inc.

p. 43: Photo © Jessie Walker Associates

p. 44: Photos © David Schrock, Basement Spaces, Inc.

p. 45: Photo © Tim Lee Photography

p. 46: Photo © Olson Photographic, LLC

p. 47: (top) Photo © David Schrock, Basement Spaces, Inc.; (bottom) Photo © Carolyn I. Bates Photography

p. 48: Photo © Roger Turk, Northlight Photography

p. 49: Photo © Steve Vierra Photography

p. 50: Photo © Mark Lohman Photography

p. 51: Photo © Peter Krupenye; architect: Carol Kurth Architects

p. 52: Photo © Jessie Walker Associates

p. 53: Photos © Olson Photographic, LLC

p. 54: (top) Photo © David Schrock, Basement Spaces, Inc.; (bottom) Photo © Randy O'Rourke

p. 55: (left) Photo © Mark Samu, Samu Studios, Inc.; (top right) Photo © Olson Photographic, LLC; (bottom right) Photo © Todd Caverly

Ch. 3

p. 56: Photo © Peter Krupenye, Carol Kurth Architects

p. 58: Photos © Gary Easter PHOTOgraphics

p. 59: Photo © Alise O'Brien Photography

pp. 60–61: Photos © Ken Gutmaker

p. 62: Photo © Beth Singer Photography, iContact Designs, Inc.

p. 63: Photo © J. H. Peterson; designers: Val Stuessi and Michal Crosby Interiors, CKD of Crystal Kitchen Center, Inc.

p. 64: (left) Photo © Grey Crawford; (top right) Photo © Philip Clayton-Thompson; (bottom right) Photo © Ken Gutmaker

p. 65: (left) Photo © Eric Roth Photography; (right) Photo by Daniel Morrison, © The Taunton Press, Inc.

p. 66: Photo © Alise O'Brien Photography

p. 67: (top) Photo © Olson Photographic, LLC; (bottom) Photo © James Ray Spahn

p. 68: Photo © Mark Samu, Samu Studios, Inc.

p. 69: (top & bottom right) Photos © David Schrock, Basement Spaces, Inc.

pp. 70–71: Photos © Sylvain Côté, Absolute Remodeling, Inc.

p. 72: Photo © Tom McWilliam

p. 73: Photo © Olson Photographic, LLC

p. 74: (top) Photo © Beth Singer Photography, iContact Designs, Inc.; (bottom) Photo © Olson Photographic, LLC

p. 75: (top right) Photo © Mark Samu, Samu Studios, Inc.; (bottom right) Photo © Mark Lohman Photography; (left) Photo by Roe A. Osborn, © The Taunton Press, Inc.

p. 76: (top) Photo © David Schrock, Basement Spaces, Inc.; (bottom) Photo © J. H. Peterson, designers Val Stuessi and Michal Crosby Interiors, CKD of Crystal Kitchen Center, Inc.

p. 77: (top) Photo © Randy O'Rourke; (bottom) Photo © Jessie Walker Associates

p. 78: (left) Photo © Jessie Walker Associates; (right) Photo by Charles Miller, © The Taunton Press, Inc.

p. 79: (top right) Photo © Lee Anne White Photography; (bottom right) Photo © Roger Turk, Northlight Photography, Inc.; (top left) Photo © Greg Premu Photography; (bottom left) Photo © Rob Karosis

p. 80 (top) © Anne Gummerson Photography; (botom) Photo © Eric Roth Photography

81: Photos © Anne Gummerson Photography

p. 82: Photos courtesy Bombay Company

p. 83: (top left & right) Photos courtesy Trinity Tables; (bottom left) Photo courtesy Restoration Hardware; (bottom right) Photo courtesy Thomasville

p. 84: (left) Photo © David Schrock, Basement Spaces, Inc.; (right) Photo © Grey Crawford

p. 85: (right) Photo © Steve Vierra Photography

p. 86: (top right) Photo © Jolynn Johnson; (bottom left) Photo © Mark Lohman Photography; (middle) Photo © Grey Crawford

p. 87: (top) Photo © David Schrock, Basement Spaces, Inc.; (bottom) Photo © Anne Gummerson Photography

p. 88: (left) Photo © Eric Roth Photography; (right) Photo © Olson Photographic, LLC

p. 90: Photo © James Ray Spahn

p. 91: Photo © Olson Photographic, LLC

p. 92: Photo by Charles Bickford, © The Taunton Press, Inc.

p. 93: Photos © Dean Della Ventura

p. 94: Photo © Olson Photographic, LLC

p. 95: Photo © Roger Turk, Northlight Photography, Inc.

p. 96: Photo © Mark Lohman Photography

p. 98: Photo © Anne Gummerson Photography

p. 99: Photo © Tim Lee Photography

pp. 100–101: Photos © Mark Lohman Photography

Ch. 4

p. 102: Photo © Mark Lohman Photography

p. 104: Photo © Tim Street-Porter

p. 105: Photo © Eric Roth Photography

pp. 106–107: (top) Photo © Roger Turk, Northlight Photography, Inc.; (bottom) Photo © Eric Roth Photography

p. 108: Photo courtesy Basement Systems, Inc., Harold Shapiro, photographer

p. 109: (top) Photo © David Schrock, Basement Spaces Inc.; (bottom) Photo © Rich Hammer

p. 110: Photo © Mark Lohman Photography

p. 111: Photo © Mark Samu, Samu Studios, Inc.

pp. 112–113: Photos © Joseph Kugielsky

p. 114: (top) Photo © Peter Vanderwarker; designer: LDa Architects, LLP; (bottom) Photo © Peter Krupenye; designer: Carol Kurth Architects

p. 115: Photo © James Carrier

p. 116: Photo © Greg Premru

p. 117: (top) Photo © Mark Lohman Photography; (bottom) Photo © Gary Easter PHOTOgraphics

pp. 118–119: Photos © David Schrock, Basement Spaces, Inc.

p. 120: (top & right) Photos © Alise O'Brien Photography; (bottom) Photo © Ken Gutmaker

pp. 122–123: Photos © Tom McWilliam

p. 124: (top) Photo © Mark Lohman Photography; (bottom) Photo © Lisa Romerein Photography

p. 125: Photo courtesy Michelle Rohrer-Lauer, photo by Barry Dave Photography

p. 126: (top & bottom left) Photos © David Schrock, Basement Spaces, Inc.; (top right) Photo © Wendell T. Weber; (bottom right) Photo © Alise O'Brien Photography

p. 128: (top) Photo © Grey Crawford; (bottom) Photo © Marc Scholtes; designer: Val Stuessi, CKD of Crystal Kitchen Center, Inc., and Michal Crosby Interiors

p. 129: Photos © Lee Anne White Photography

p. 130: (bottom) Photo © Randy O'Rourke; (right) Photo © Steve Vierra Photography

p. 132: (left) Photo © Mark Samu, Samu Studios, Inc.; (right) Photo © Todd Caverly

p. 133: (right) Photo © Randy O'Rourke

p. 134: Photo © Todd Caverly

p. 135: Photo © Randy O'Rourke

Ch. 5

p. 136: Photo © Eric Roth Photography

p. 138: (top) Photo © Olson Photographic, LLC; (bottom) Photo © Roger Turk, Northlight Photograpy, Inc.

p. 139: Photo © Jessie Walker Associates

p. 140–141: Photos © Steve Vierra Photography

p. 143: (top left) Photo © Mark Lohman Photography; (bottom left & right) Photos © David Schrock, Basement Spaces, Inc.

p. 144: Photo © davidduncanlivingston.com

p. 145: Photo © Mark Lohman Photography

p. 146: Photo by Michael Pekovich, © The Taunton Press, Inc.

p. 148: (top) Photo © Roger Turk, Northlight Photography, Inc.; (bottom) Photo © Susan Gilmore

p. 149: Photo © Mark Samu, Samu Studios, Inc.

p. 150: (top) Photo © Roger Turk, Northlight Photography, Inc.; (bottom) Photo © David Schrock, Basement Spaces, Inc.

p. 151: Photo © Brian Vanden Brink

p. 152: (top) Photo © Eric Roth Photography; (bottom) Photo © Steve Vierra Photography

p. 153: (left) Photo © Eric Roth Photography; (top right) Photo courtesy Sylvania; (bottom right) Photo © Evan Sklar

p. 154: (top) Photo © Mark Lohman Photography; (bottom) Photo © Carolyn I. Bates Photography

p. 155: Photo © James Ray Spahn

p. 156: (top) Photo © Eric Roth Photography; (bottom) Photo © Carolyn I. Bates Photography

p. 157: Photo © Beth Singer Photograpy; designer: iContact Designs, Inc.

p. 158: Photo © Olson Photographic, LLC

p 159: Photos © David Schrock, Basement Spaces, Inc.

p. 160: (top) Photo © Jessie Walker Associates; (bottom) Photo © Olson Photographic, LLC

p. 161: Photo © Lee Anne White Photography

p. 162: (left) Photo © Todd Caverly; (right) Photo © Tim Street-Porter

p. 163: (top right) Photo © David Schrock, Basement Spaces, Inc.; (bottom right) Photo © Grey Crawford

p. 164–165: Photos © Sylvain Côté, Absolute Remodeling, Inc.

p. 166: Photo © davidduncanlivingston.com

p. 167: (top) Photo © Mark Lohman Photography; (bottom) Photo © Grey Crawford

p. 168–169: Photos © Mark Samu, Samu Studios, Inc.

p. 170: (left) Photo courtesy Carole Fabrics; (top right) Photo © Carolyn I. Bates Photography; (bottom right) Photo © David Schrock, Basement Spaces, Inc.

p. 171: (top) Photo © David Schrock, Basement Spaces, Inc.; (bottom) Photo © Jessie Walker Associates

INDEX

MORE GREAT IDEAS THAT REALLY WORK

KITCHEN IDEAS THAT WORK

Beth Veillette
Paperback
ISBN 13: 978-156158-837-4
ISBN10: 1-56158-837-7
EAN: 9781561588374
9 x 10½
240 pages
382 full color photographs
  throughout
27 drawings
Product # 070883
$19.95 U.S., $25.95 Can.
Available

DECORATING IDEAS THAT WORK

Heather J. Paper
Paperback
ISBN 13: 978-156158-950-0
ISBN10: 1-56158-950-0
EAN: 9781561589500
9 x 10½
288 pages
475 full color photographs
  throughout
30 drawings
Product # 070962
$21.95 U.S., $27.95 Can.
Available October 2007

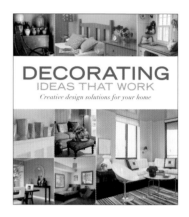

BATHROOM IDEAS THAT WORK

Scott Gibson
Paperback
ISBN 13: 978-156158-836-7
ISBN10: 1-56158-836-9
EAN: 9781561588367
9 x 10½
224 pages
367 full color photographs
  throughout
17 drawings
Product # 070884
$19.95 U.S., $25.95 Can.
Available

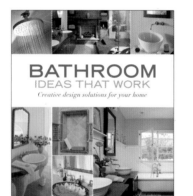

OUTDOOR KITCHEN IDEAS THAT WORK

Lee Anne White
Paperback
ISBN 13: 978-156158-958-6
ISBN10: 1-56158-958-6
EAN: 9781561589586
9 x 10½
224 pages
350 full color photographs
  throughout
30 drawings
Product # 070968
$19.95 U.S., $25.95 Can.
Available January 2008

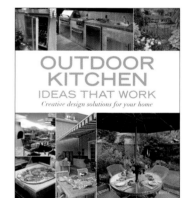